a guide
to participation

a guide
to participation

field work,
role playing cases,
and other forms

JOHN C. BOLLENS
university of california, los angeles

DALE ROGERS MARSHALL
university of california, davis

Prentice-Hall, Inc., *Englewood Cliffs, New Jersey*

Library of Congress Catalog Card No.: 72–12537

ISBN: C 0–13–370577–3
      P 0–13–370569–2

Printed in the United States of America

10 9 8 7 6 5 4 3 2 1

Prentice-Hall International, Inc., *London*
Prentice-Hall of Australia, Pty. Ltd., *Sydney*
Prentice-Hall of Canada, Ltd., *Toronto*
Prentice-Hall of India Private Limited, *New Delhi*
Prentice-Hall of Japan, Inc., *Tokyo*

contents

4   how to do work in the field, 43

5   analyzing and using the results, 59

6   sample field work projects, 71

introduction to role playing cases, 87

7   a state as negotiator in a medical school controversy: the national government, a city, a medical school, and the black community, 90

preface

In working with students we have long felt a need for a guide to encourage participation in "real life" situations as part of an individual's education. We are speaking broadly of participation to mean involvement in a wide variety of activities and projects—public and private, national, state, and local—generally in areas where people live. This book is such a guide.

Two types of educational participation are emphasized: field work, which is participation in social research, and role playing, which allows participation in controversies arising when people take part in social systems. These two types are part of the broader subject of participation considered in chapter 1. The traditional and newer patterns of social and political participation, which are discussed in this introductory chapter, are directly related to field work and role playing cases. They furnish significant topics for the former and valuable background information for the latter. In turn, field work and role playing cases help people to develop greater competence for taking part in these other participatory forms.

Both the field work and the role playing cases described in this book view the "real world" as a promising laboratory, a resource often ignored in favor of library research and abstract discussions of society, which seems to exist somewhere out in space. Emphasis on such research and discussion is ironic because the geographical community in which people live is such an obvious place to start attempts to understand social and political systems, whether national, state, or local. It is real, tangible, and difficult to avoid; we rub elbows with it everyday. Furthermore, any locality is so tied to larger governmental, social, and economic systems that it provides many insights into them without having to make long junkets to Washington, D.C., or other distant centers. For example, state and national leaders come to many localities for hearings, conferences, and business meetings; and state and national agencies also have field offices in many areas of the country.

This book focuses on domestic issues involving private social and economic groups, political and governmental organizations, and efforts at all levels that are common to the locations of most people in the United States. Consequently this publication should be useful for courses in political science, sociology, economics, planning, social work, public health, and other fields. The book is primarily designed as a supplemental text to complement a variety of substantive topics. It will guide students in related field work and cases and thus increase their participation in the issues raised in the courses. In the absence of a guide such as this one many instructors have felt they could not take time away from the substantive material to discuss field work methods or develop case experiences. We hope the availability of this student guide will lessen the amount of time the instructor needs to commit to participatory mechanics and will increase the participatory benefits for the students.

After the discussion of participation in general in the first chapter, chapters 2 through 6 describe how to do field work, by which we mean an extended self-designed project on some aspect of American society involving participation in a real life situation and an analysis of that participatory experience. Separate chapters consider how to formulate a topic for such a project, design methods for obtaining information, implement these plans, and analyze the data collected. The final chapter in this section presents some sample field projects. We believe that most instructors prefer a single major field project in a semester or a quarter, and we have kept this idea in mind in developing these chapters. Field work lets each person fit his activities to his interests and abilities. It is exhilarating to watch the energy, imagination, and initiative unleashed when people pursue a significant self-defined project about which they really care.

Direct personal contact with actual social processes makes formerly abstract issues and concepts come to life. Exposure to real complexities tests intellectual positions, and emerging convictions have more depth because they are based on experience outside one's supportive circle of friends. Field work may also establish contacts the individual will want to pursue later for action purposes, careers, or friendships. And field work if done well can add to the individual's knowledge of social process, and this information can in turn contribute to changing the process. For example, one student's paper on the operation of a state professional licensing board was used by some board members as evidence in their campaign to reform that board.

Chapters 7 through 11 present five role playing cases, based on actual situations, which illustrate conflicts occurring when citizens participate in social issues. The controversies include the location of a medical school, the control of a war on poverty agency and a police department, the autonomy of teachers, the financing of rapid transit, and the structure and powers of regional government for a metropolis.

Although these cases are organized in a role playing format, they are not restricted to that interesting use. They may be employed as "readings" for different purposes. For instance, using this option, the instructor might have classroom discussions of how the students would deal with the conflicts. He might have students do written appraisals of various phases of the cases, or he might use the materials to give the students adequate background for his analysis of particular concepts contained in them. Regardless of how they are used, the cases are also valuable as preparation for field work, alerting people to issues worth pursuing and things to watch for when they are in the field.

Introductions preceding chapters 2 and 7 respectively explain the field work and the role playing cases in more detail. These two types of educational experiences reflect the interest in participation characteristic of our era and also can contribute to the gradual emergence of understanding and norms appropriate to a society being challenged by demands for extended participation.

We wish to express our appreciation to Biliana Ambrecht, Mark Bruckner, Jane Feldman, James Gleason, Joan Machlis, Kay Martin, Joyce Mitchell, William Muir, and Francine Rabinovitz, who kindly commented on the manuscript before its publication, and to Carolyn Davidson and Joan Lee of Prentice-Hall, who capably saw us through the various stages of the book's production.

*a guide
to participation*

introduction to participation

1

Participation has become an important issue in American society. It is a topic of debate in groups covering the entire political spectrum and operating in many different circumstances. All of us are familiar with the conflicts in the university between students and administrations and in the community between minorities and officials of public and private agencies. But we have heard less about the parallel controversies in professional societies between local branches and the national organization. For example, local associations within the American Public Health Association have demanded a larger voice in the national group. Governmental agencies such as the Department of Health, Education and Welfare and the State Department are also experiencing arguments between personnel at the bottom and at the top of the hierarchies about the distribution of participation and power.

In all these settings participation is a recurring topic of many dimensions. What does participation mean—advice or control? Who should participate—all interested parties or only the most highly qualified? How much participation is desirable and when and where? Should participation come only after a proposal has been prepared or throughout the process of developing one? What effect will the different types of participation have?

This interest in citizen participation is significantly affecting our social system and our understanding of that system. One result has been renewed emphasis on educational practices involving participation. Appreciation of citizen participation has been accompanied by increased concern for student participation in education. Just as old forms of social and political participation are being challenged, so too are traditional pedagogical techniques. Both educators and students are questioning mere absorption of information in courses and are increasingly judging such courses as woefully inadequate. Awareness is growing that active involvement in the learning process stimulates meaningful learning.

Two types of educational experiences based on participation—field work and role playing cases—can stimulate active involvement in thinking about important social issues. Field work requires participation in an experience and analysis of that participatory experience. Role playing cases consist of student participation in classroom reenactments of problems arising when citizen participation leads to conflict. Field work and role playing cases are forms of participation contributing to knowledge and skills, which increase effectiveness in other forms of participation.

Other forms of participation, discussed in this chapter, may become topics for field work and provide background for the cases. Because field work and role playing are only two of many kinds of participation, they need to be viewed as part of the whole topic of participation. To accomplish this purview, we shall first review the traditional patterns of social and political participation, then consider newer patterns, and finally summarize the arguments in the debate about the latter.

TRADITIONAL PATTERNS

The current debate about participation must not obscure the fact that it is not a new issue. Participation is both an ancient and a contemporary theme. Social philosophers as early as Plato and Aristotle have discussed how much voice the citizen should have in the state. And even though democratic political theory is based on individuals' possessing a voice in government, ideas about which individuals and how much voice have changed throughout history, generally in the direction of broadening participation. Government by the people once meant that monarchs had to give some power to nobles. Later it meant that property holding adult white males could participate in the election of leaders. Still later the franchise was widened in the United States to include nonproperty holders, then adult Negro males, then all adult females, and recently with the lowering of the age of adulthood all persons over eighteen. Who can participate is not all that has changed; how people can participate has also been modified. Participation once meant voting for officials. Subsequently the reform movement in the early part of the twentieth century widened participation to include voting directly on legislation by initiative and referendum procedures.

The norms of American society have always encouraged participation in social and political activities. For example, public schools stress the value of participating in voluntary organizations and political activities. Alexis de Tocqueville and many others have characterized Americans as joiners (*Democracy in America,* vol. II, p. 106). A review of social science studies of American participation patterns—who participates and how they do so—shows the traditional forms of social and political participation. (For additional details, see Lester Milbrath, *Political Participation;* Robert Lane, *Political Life;* and Dale Marshall, "Who Participates in What?" *)

First, what do we know about who participates? Wide support exists for the proposition that participation varies according to the socio-economic status (SES) of the individual. Hence people with higher SES (higher educational and occupational attainment) are more likely to participate in formal social organizations and political activities than lower SES individuals. Participation in formal voluntary organizations also appears to be related strongly to political participation, independent of SES. That is, if an individual is active in voluntary organizations, he is likely to participate in political activities regardless of his SES. Studies of working-class individuals typically find participation in informal rather than formal organizations. But little attention had been given to ethnic variations in participation.

Second, what do we know about how people participate—what kinds of organizations do they join and how active do they become? Studies of social participation show that different classes of people join different types of organizations, but these studies only make broad distinctions between types of groups. For example, middle and upper SES groups typically join civic and service organizations, whereas lower and working-class people usually join churches, fraternal, social, recreational, or work-related groups. Civic and service organizations, including such groups as Rotary, Parent-Teacher Association, Scouts, Community Chest, Chamber of Commerce, and Junior League, have the most members.

Distinctions are often made among forms of participation according to the amount of activity involved. The least active type of participation involves exposing oneself to stimuli, followed in turn by joining an organization, attending activities, contributing money or time to activities, planning and soliciting support for activities, and finally seeking and

* Full citations to all references in the various chapters are presented in the bibliographical section at the end of the book.

holding leadership positions. These levels of activities apply to participation in both social and political organizations. And in both types the less active forms of participation are most prevalent.

Levels of participation in political organizations have been singled out for particular attention. Milbrath (p. 18) presents the following hierarchy of political involvement, with the least frequent behavior at the top of the list and the most frequent at the bottom.

Holding public and party office
Being a candidate for office
Soliciting political funds
Attending a caucus or a strategy meeting
Becoming an active member in a political party
Contributing time to a political campaign
Attending a political meeting or rally
Making a monetary contribution to a party or candidate
Contacting a public official or a political leader
Wearing a button or putting a sticker on a car
Attempting to talk another into voting a certain way
Initiating a political discussion
Voting
Exposing oneself to political stimuli

Several omissions from these traditional forms are revealing. Note that the activities focus on elections and political parties—that is, on organizations attempting to influence the electoral process. No mention is made of participation designed to formulate policy by administrative agencies or legislatures or to implement policy by public agencies. Milbrath (p. 18) specifically acknowledges the other omission—participation that bypasses the established political channels, such as protest demonstrations, general strikes, civil disobedience, and coups d'etat.

EMERGING PATTERNS

Although participation is an old topic and many traditional forms exist, we are in the midst of a new burst of interest in the subject. Traditional participation in both social and political organizations is being questioned and new patterns are emerging, which expand participation to new participants and increase the significance of certain types of participation.

Why has participation become a rallying cry? Terrence Cook and

Patrick Morgan point out in *Participatory Democracy* (pp. 3–4) that demands for participation are most intense when the franchise has been most widely extended and when merit appointments for administrators are most firmly established. The trend toward centralization of power in elected officials and appointed experts has paralleled the growth of a complex technological society and governments as the latter have become responsible for more activities. As a result, people have come to feel that government and social institutions are distant and cannot be influenced by most individuals. Pleas for participation constitute an attempt to reverse this trend toward individual powerlessness.

Participation demands are a challenge to the powerholders, to the elected and appointed officials, to the professionals, and to the established forms of participation. The demands reflect a desire to make social institutions and government more responsive by decentralizing them, by bringing the sources of power closer to the people. Although they have this much in common, the demands are deceptive: common language often hides vastly different opinions about who should participate, how they should participate, and why participation is desirable.

Let us look at the emerging patterns of participation. Who are the new participants? The new people are those formerly inactive in social and political organizations, most noticeably low SES individuals and ethnic groups. Many governmental programs have stimulated this participation by requiring that recipients be involved in planning and implementing poverty, model cities, housing, health, and education programs. Enabling legislation for all these programs requires participation by the clients—the poor, the blacks, and the browns who typically had low rates of social and political participation. The legislation is often vague, with interesting differences in the requirements, but the theme of participation is striking (Melvin Mogulof, *Citizen Participation*). It is too early to tell whether the resulting programs will actually change the traditional patterns of who participates. But indications are that more organizations of the poor have been created. As they have attempted to gain influence in government programs, minority groups have organized and gained experience in defending their interests and have joined more organizations.

The increased participation of low SES individuals and ethnic groups has been accompanied by activation of other groups which had not commonly been participants. People at the bottom of many different organizations or social systems—students, blue-collar workers, younger members of professional groups and public agencies, and rank and file policemen—now show signs of increased participation. People at the bottom now feel freer to question people at the top, to express critical opinions; they expect people at the top to take their interests into account.

An important example of people at the bottom becoming active participants is the successful passage of legislation allowing eighteen-year-olds to vote.

What changes are taking place in the kinds of organizations people are joining and in their participation? People are participating in a much wider range of organizations. The list of organizations used in traditional surveys of participation—Rotary, Scouts, and so on—is outdated today. These traditional surveys emphasized established nationwide organizations. No mention was made of local ad hoc groups that spring up to achieve a specific goal, to take action on a certain issue—groups organized, for instance, to start a community health clinic or a volunteer tutorial project, to take a civil rights action, or to oppose the location of a proposed freeway or expressway. Many new organizations of this type have come into existence (Ralph Nader, *Action for a Change* and The O. M. Collective, *The Organizer's Manual*). Membership in such grass roots organizations may now equal that in traditional civic and service groups.

People are also participating in more diverse types of political activity. Political participation no longer means primarily participation in elections and political parties. People want to shape policy directly and not merely select officials who will shape it. Thus many social organizations have become politicized; that is, they take stands on public policy issues and actively attempt to influence policy. In other words they have increased their lobbying activities. For instance, many community groups such as free clinics and professional groups like policemen have become active advocates of policies they feel will further their interests. Although lobbying is not a new political activity, such action is becoming more widespread as more and more groups are engaging in it.

Another type of political participation of growing importance is involvement in administration. Lobbying efforts characteristically have focused on legislatures and elected executive leaders. But the tremendous growth in administrative agencies and their importance in formulating and implementing policies have stimulated more people to want to gain access to these agencies. Lobbying now aims at influencing administrative agencies as well as legislatures. Furthermore, groups are not content to participate in administration only as lobbyists; they insist on direct participation in the agencies. Such participation is not new. For years, agricultural agencies, for example, have involved farmers, and regulatory agencies have included representatives of the regulated groups. But now new groups are asking for direct participation in administration. Although such kinds of political participation are not novel, in recent years the amount of participation in certain forms has increased greatly as formerly excluded groups have started doing what select groups have been doing for a long time—lobbying in legislatures and administrative agencies and attempting to participate directly in administrative agencies.

Because we cannot discuss all the changes in participation, we have selected some changes that seem most significant. Yet even those vary in who participates and how they participate. The diversity of the changes makes generalization particularly difficult, so in the following discussion of forms of participation we limit the topic even further. We will only consider participation in administrative agencies (public and private), distinguished according to who participates and how much they participate. We suggest a continuum that extends from a narrow to a broad range of participants giving only advice and then proceeds from a narrow to a broad range of participants sharing formal power.

The first form may be called advocacy. This role may be filled by regular administrators in existing jobs. The role requires active support rather than neutral competence, taking positions and defending them. People who favor the advocacy role assume that the advocate will take the side of the clients or the powerless. Thus lawyers who talk of advocacy law are referring to attorneys who help consumers or welfare recipients; and planners who speak of advocacy planning are referring to planners who take the side of conservationists (the assumption being that other, more powerful interests have always had their advocates). The advocacy role rejects the view that administrators should be neutral experts who merely carry out decisions made by elected officials without letting personal value preferences interfere. In contrast the neutrality role has called, for instance, for city planners to explore objectively the implications of various alternatives and present them to the decision-makers rather than try to sell the alternative they personally prefer. The new interest in participation we have been describing has led to challenges of the neutral competence view (Herbert Kaufman, "Administrative Decentralization and Political Power"). Many administrators now reject it on two grounds: first, neutrality is an illusion, since administrators' values always influence their judgments, which should be made explicit, and, second, excessive emphasis on neutrality leads to unresponsiveness.

A second form of participation may be called new careers. These are new jobs in existing organizations filled by new people who have not traditionally participated in them. The idea is to create new jobs that will enable a greater diversity of types of people to participate in organizations. The jobs are paraprofessional positions concerned with assisting teachers, social workers, medical personnel, and other professionals, particularly in their relations with clients and the community.

A third form of participation may be called advice giving. This role involves asking new people to advise the organization. Advisory participation may occur in many different arrangements: any subsection of an organization can create advisory committees to assist with its programs. The number of such committees has proliferated rapidly in public programs such as poverty, model cities, health, housing, and crime and in private activities, including those carried out by the Young Women's Christian Association.

The three forms described all involve amounts of participation that stop short of formal participation in power. The advocate, the paraprofessional, and the advisor may influence how an organization operates, but the amount of influence depends entirely on the acquiescence of the rest of the organization.

Let us look now at forms of administrative participation that involve a greater amount of participation—change in the distribution of power. The first form is administrative decentralization, whereby the location of power within the organization is moved downward in the hierarchy. This relocation of power can occur without any change in jobs or in people filling them; the power of a particular position is merely increased. For instance, decentralization may mean that a field office director can gain control over the allocation of funds among units within his office rather than such decisions being made at higher levels.

The second form is shared power whereby power is decentralized all the way down to the clients of the organization, who are brought into its decisionmaking. Typically the clients are made members of organizational policy boards, which have formal responsibility for planning and implementation. For example, poverty representatives are placed on community action agency boards, which are responsible for the operation of poverty programs.

The third form of administrative participation is called community control, radical decentralization, or participatory democracy. Here power is decentralized more completely; power is substantially devolved to groups of clients; they are not merely brought into an organization where they have to share power with others. In this form clients set up the organization and have a large measure of control over certain functions. Thus community school boards might be established within a large school system and given considerable authority over teachers and curriculum. This form of participation is at the far end of the decentralization continuum we have been discussing, and involves participants in the most active form of participation. It usually necessitates formation of small units. Paradoxically this means that demands for participation, which reflect the feeling that we have too much government, can produce more rather than fewer public organizations. Moreover, this form multiplies small units precisely when many analysts are concluding that existing governmental jurisdictions are generally too small to meet certain problems, such as air and water pollution, in a large interdependent society (Terrence Cook and Patrick Morgan, *Participatory Democracy*, p. 29). It also multiplies organizations when some analysts feel pluralism has already gone too far; that is, too many competing groups are already present in our society (Theodore Lowi, *The End of Liberalism*).

Despite such complications, the demands for community control are multiplying. Participation seems to lead to demands for more control. Typically advisory councils want to advance to the sharing of power, and clients on shared power groups push for greater amounts of power. But community control forms of participation use diverse strategies of operation. One strategy is called locality development or social service. Groups controlled by residents try to mobilize a community to carry out self-help projects. For example, community development corporations stress communication and collaboration with established groups that have scarce resources (Fred Cox, *Strategies of Community Organization*).

Another strategy used by community control groups operates outside established channels. Because their goals involve restructuring the institutions, these groups feel that working within such institutions is not possible. So they work outside the system, making demands for major changes and using mass participation to make themselves heard. Protest demonstrations, civil disobedience, and illegal acts such as destroying files or engaging in physical violence are familiar mass participation tactics. This social action or conflict strategy is widely associated with the name of Saul Alinsky, who wrote *Reveille for Radicals*. The idea is that established institutions will not change until they are pressured to do so. Conflict is used as a way of organizing the unorganized so they can obtain power to exert the pressure needed to modify institutions.

CONTROVERSY OVER NEWER FORMS

Each new form of participation can be the subject of heated debate, just as the traditional forms were when they first developed. In each organization, demands for increased participation create controversy over who should participate and how much they should take part. The arguments vary according to the setting, but certain general patterns are apparent.

The arguments in favor of increasing participation fall into two broad categories; one type is concerned with improvement in policy or in the social system and the other with improvement in individuals. The first maintains that participation can improve decisions and result in beneficial changes in social systems. Sometimes the assumption is that institutions should be responsive to clients because they know their needs best. For example, proponents of student participation say that students should have power over hiring teachers because they are the best judges of teaching ability; or welfare recipients say that if they shared power in formulating policy, welfare programs would better serve the clients' real needs. But even if one does not assume that clients know their interests, it is possible to argue that participation improves the social system because it leads to changes clients feel are in their interest. And people should know that they can make themselves heard. In this view, participation is valuable because it enables systems to adapt to new demands, and this adaptation is essential for the maintenance of system support. Note that in this sense the system changes so the individuals' attitude toward it becomes more positive.

The second argument emphasizes beneficial changes in individuals. Instead of saying that participation changes systems to fit people, the claim is that participation changes individuals to fit systems. Participation is assumed to be therapeutic, socializing the participant by increasing his knowledge, skills, and sense of personal and political effectiveness. Some proponents of participation emphasize the intrinsic values of this learning for the individual; others concentrate on the value for the social system, saying that this learning leads individuals to give more support to the system. For example, people who participate in an organization are said to feel more positively toward that organization. Thus participation is often seen as a way of engineering consent or developing support for a system by coopting potential opposition. Note that in this sense the system does not change, only the individual does.

The arguments against increased participation are the inverse of the supporting ones. Participation is said to hurt decisions. According to this view, the increased number of participants with differing opinions will result in bitter conflicts. As a consequence, decisions may be impossible or they may be compromises satisfying no one. And even if conflict is low, the decisions will be poor because the new participants are not experts. Theodore Lowi argues in *The End of Liberalism* that increased participation will simply multiply the number of interest groups with narrow views, making decisions in the public interest even more difficult. Numerous other criticisms are made of the quality of decisions when participation is increased. Participation is too inefficient because it prolongs decisionmaking and necessitates much duplication. Participation leads to diversity and inconsistency between decisionmaking units, and it may undermine values such as equity, which should take precedence over self-determination. Participation will increase fragmentation because small units are necessary for participation, but they cannot deal with problems extending beyond their jurisdiction.

Opponents of increased participation further contend that participation may not improve individuals. New participants are said to become discouraged when they realize the complexities involved in social action and become aware of their own inadequacies. Their feelings of efficacy may decrease, and instead of becoming more supportive of organizations they may become more alienated and hostile.

This brief discussion of the arguments about the new forms of participation is intended to indicate the complex issues involved in the debate. Participation should not be viewed as either a panacea or a scourge. It is too easy to form an opinion about participation without adequate thought, to label the "good guy" and the "bad guy" in the debate, according to the fashion of the moment. However, the advantages and the disadvantages of any new form of participation should be carefully weighed. Proponents' rhetoric suggests only good outcomes, whereas opponents' rhetoric suggests the reverse. Neither suggestion is reasonable; changes have both benefits and costs. In assessing a specific proposal for a new form of participation, we need to ask: Who will participate? How will they participate? What results will the new participation have for the participants and for the policy?

Answers to these questions indicate who will benefit from the proposed change and who will lose. A new form of participation can influence power distribution and modify policy; in other words the reform can change who gets what in a society. To reach a sound opinion, an individual needs to be aware of the implications a new form of participation has for power and policy.

Careful assessment is particularly necessary to protect against the alluring rhetoric of participation. Proponents of diametrically opposite schemes have used such slogans as "power to the people" and "the democratic way." For instance, community control in a wealthy suburb may mean that decisions will preserve the existing distribution of wealth; whereas community control in a ghetto may mean the reverse because new groups may get power and make decisions challenging traditional programs.

A proposed new form of participation contains assumptions about who the new participants will be and how they will change policy. Proponents think participation will be a strategy leading to a goal they desire. For example, people who demand seating more representatives of the poor on community action agency boards in the war on poverty often assume that these poverty representatives will favor more radical programs than other members. If the new representatives do not contribute to such an outcome, the proponents may lose their enthusiasm for participation. Such a change in attitude toward participation makes sense when participation is viewed as a strategy designed to achieve a certain end, often a change in who gets what. Awareness of this aspect of demands for participation should prevent naïve adherence to participation without a realization of its potentially profound impact on other values. Changes in participation are not neutral; they may have major implications for the distribution of power in a society.

This discussion of participation has not addressed the problem of how an individual decides what forms of participation he wants to pursue. Action-oriented people always want to know what kind of participation is most effective. In general it depends on the specific conditions involved. Each person must decide what resources he has, what resources other groups and individuals (both those he supports and those he wants to change) have, and what the special characteristics of the problem are. For some individuals, participation within established forms is most effective; for others participation outside those channels is more valuable. Our view is that multiple forms of participation are needed, and both traditional and new forms of participation are essential. So individuals must choose the forms that best use their resources.

The forms of participation considered in the following chapters involve participation in education. Interest in educational experiences using participation has recently increased as part of the growing general concern for all forms of participation. Even though other forms of participation have implications for the distribution of power and therefore are properly controversial, educational experiences based on participation are not designed to change policy, but to change individuals. The goal is not to make individuals more supportive of social systems or less supportive. Education is not a training ground for perpetuating or destroying the system. Rather, the process of education stimulates analysis of the system and development of personal and intellectual skills that will enable the individual to formulate and act on his beliefs. The goal is to enable people to learn in the most effective way. Teachers typically find that they learn more as educators than they did as students, because they must actively think and perform. This observation supports the belief that people learn best when they participate in their own education. Too often students sit passively in an audience, relaxed spectators at least until the traumatic experience of an examination, which often requires simply tossing back the thinking done earlier by the teacher.

Educational experiences based on participation can cause anxiety even among those who call the loudest for participation. Since admittedly we have all been socialized to some degree into the traditional educational roles, cultural shock seems inevitable when the call comes to participate. The realization that educational participation takes more work may lead to resentment. Sitting back is easier, but also less interesting and worthwhile.

introduction to
field work

The field work section of this book is written in the belief that one of the best ways to learn about American society is to participate in it. And when this participation occurs as part of systematic inquiry, its value is heightened because one learns not only what is going on but also how to think about a complex reality, to ask worthwhile questions, to deal with the questions, and to reach conclusions about appropriate personal action.

Because we feel it is so valuable to "get into the field," we have not attempted to write a methodological treatise dealing with the complexities of the scientific method. Instead we have discussed only those processes we think are essential to worthwhile field projects. Field work experience is an excellent way to learn about empirical social science. It leads to an appreciation of other people's studies and a desire to learn more about methodology. Early exposure to field work prevents the problem of premature sophistication that arises in abstract methodology courses if students learn to mimic jargon and procedures without developing an interest in or a feel for the realities the jargon and procedures were created to handle. But field work can provide a sound basis for abstraction and for appreciation of methodological intricacies.

The lack of field work in many courses has often been due to the absence of procedural guides. Methodological texts and workbooks have been written, as have activist tracts and pleas for citizen involvement in a wide variety of locality-based activities. Until now, however, there have been no guidelines on how to integrate such experiences into an intellectual framework and how to bridge the gap between experience and analysis. Field work supplies the material for accomplishing these objectives.

The field work section of this book is directed to instructors committed to intellectual inquiry and suspicious about the value of mere exposure to experience and the rhetoric of involvement. It is also directed to students doubtful about abstractions in isolation but desirous of a chance to think about their experiences and to fit them into an analytical framework. We try to give the participants sufficient skills and confidence to take advantage of the myriad field work opportunities, to develop such experiences to fit their needs, and to integrate these experiences into their lives.

choosing a topic

2

Before attempting to design a field work project, we need to be clear about what field work is. Most students are familiar with library research but not with empirical inquiry. Library research involves synthesizing other people's ideas. For instance, the student finds what others have written on a topic such as educational innovation and uses their ideas to develop his ideas. He has no firsthand experience with the subject; neither does he develop new evidence, even though the conclusions he reaches may be original. In contrast, field work requires direct personal contact with the phenomenon and the development of new evidence.

Since not all topics lend themselves to this kind of exploration, careful attention must be given to designing projects that are compatible with empirical inquiry. One important step is to formulate a problem that can be dealt with by evidence. Questions of fact can be answered by empirical evidence, but questions of value cannot. For example, it is not possible to collect evidence relevant to the question of whether a city government should be replaced by a metropolitan government. The question needs to be transformed into subquestions with factual components to be handled by empirical inquiry. Such subquestions might be: Is the current city government achieving its goals? What are the alternative forms for achieving the goals more effectively? Would such forms be feasible in the city under consideration? Thus

17

to do empirical research one must find factual aspects of any topic of interest, aspects about which pertinent evidence is obtainable. This point does not imply that normative questions cannot serve as the basis of field work. Some of the best field work arises from an interest in normative questions such as: What is the desirable balance between liberty and equality? Who should rule? How responsible should the rulers be? But a normative question must be reformulated so that it has empirical components.

Another important step in designing projects is to narrow a general topic so it becomes a focused question that can be dealt with manageably. Because this selection process is so important and so easily overlooked, we shall discuss it in detail.

FORMULATING GENERAL TOPICS

Many strategies can be followed in choosing research topics. The second part of this book (Chapters 7 through 11), which discusses participation in social systems, suggests a wide range of appropriate topics. Students may also find ideas in course syllabi, readings, bibliographical citations in readings, current magazines, and newspapers. Brainstorming sessions can generate many general topics. For example, a group interested in urban problems responded to the question, What do we want to find out more about?, by constructing the following list in simply a few minutes: Who works in local political parties? How should a group be organized to lobby effectively? How well does racial integration work in the schools? How effective are letter writing campaigns in influencing the political process? What percentage of people in disadvantaged areas vote and why? What makes a person an effective agent of change? How does racism affect community action in disadvantaged areas? Do the schools really need more money, and if so, what are the possible sources of revenue? How can the media coverage of the city be improved? Why isn't something being done to end pollution in this city? How should welfare programs be changed? What goes on in a legislator's office? What can a person with a complaint against the police do to obtain justice? How does the county governing board reach decisions? What image do people in different circumstances have of this community?

After the brainstorming, the group was divided into small groups, each taking one of the general questions and investigating ways to narrow the issue into specific questions suitable for field work. Before describing the results, we should consider several observations about the original list. The general questions are already more specific than some students are used to; they may be accustomed to writing papers about a general topic such as political parties, interest groups, or integration. Such work too often results in a rambling list of facts. Of course, many times when students first think about a topic, they start with a general heading, but then they must ask themselves, What do we want to know about this heading? When they can formulate their area of interest as a general question, they are at the general topic level illustrated in the brainstorming example. But this level is still much too broad for probing field work. To answer each general question would require years of work and several volumes of findings, or it could lead to a vague response that merely repeats current conventional wisdom. Students trying to handle such a general question often end up superficially summarizing available library material and tacking on quotes from field work interviews. But this formal adherence to field work requirements does not make a strong field project.

NARROWING TO SPECIFIC QUESTIONS

How does one arrive at a question that leads to satisfying field work? This process may be illustrated by showing how the previously mentioned brainstorming group narrowed the general questions it formulated. Its members were asked to make the general questions into specific questions suitable for field work, by thinking of all the subquestions included in the topic and all the ways the general questions could be broken into more manageable parts. The small group working on pollution devised the following suggestions for narrowing the question, Why isn't something being done to end pollution in this city? Aspects that could contribute to answering the general question were: What public (federal, state, regional, and local) and private groups are concerned with the various types of pollution? What are they trying to do about the problem? What powers do they have? How do they operate? What support for and obstacles to their efforts exist in the community? What do they think should be done? Background research may be necessary to narrow a general question into specific components.

EXPLORING IMPLICATIONS OF SPECIFIC QUESTIONS

Before the individual researcher selects a specific question as the focus of his project, he should weigh the possible results of working on each particular question. Several considerations may enter into this exploration:

1. What kinds of field work could answer the question? How can evidence be gathered to deal with the question? What needs to be observed, what files read, and what people interviewed?
2. How feasible is this work? How accessible are the necessary sources of information? Are time and mobility adequate for obtaining the available information?
3. How interested is the researcher in the work called for by the question? Would the experience contribute to his educational growth? Would it bring him into contact with people and material he has been wanting to work with? Would it lead to future academic or action projects of interest?
4. How significant would the findings be? Does the question have greater implications? For example, a study of who controls zoning in a given community could be a fruitful way of dealing with the larger question of who rules.

This aspect of research is often hardest to evaluate, especially for a beginner to a field of study. The researcher must decide what he expects to find out and whether such results would be interesting or merely busywork. For example, simply listing the organizations concerned with pollution may be duplicating already available work. The criterion of significance will vary; sometimes the emphasis will be on the scholarly caliber of research, while other times the primary concern will be its educational value for the researcher so if the work is new to him it need not also be an original contribution to the field.

Field work requires realism. Careful attention to these considerations can help prevent the selection of dead-end projects, which prove to be impossible, uninteresting, or unenlightening. Many social scientists have periods while working on projects when they become discouraged and feel such adjectives could properly be applied to their work. But careful advance planning can help them weather these periods and produce worthwhile results. (For interesting descriptions of the personal side of social research, see Phillip Hammond, ed., *Sociologists at Work*, and Arthur Vidich and others, *Reflections on Community Studies*.)

CHOOSING A SPECIFIC QUESTION

After exploring the implications of specific questions, the whole issue of project choice should be reconsidered. It is not possible to devote time to all the questions that interest the researcher, and choosing one is not easy. As one person said, "Population, pollution, poverty, racism—each topic is supposedly of utmost importance, but I cannot drop everything and become totally committed to all of them, so how can I decide what to do?" Despite the difficulty, the individual must decide which general topic and related specific question is most significant, interesting, and feasible for him.

Selection of field work offers an opportunity to shape a project that will allow a student to pursue his educational goals. Unfortunately some students have become so discouraged by the frustrations in education that they resign themselves merely to going through the motions of taking courses. When assigned a field work project they ask, What does the teacher want? But the proper question is, How can I fit this project to my educational needs? Field work allows students to design meaningful learning experiences. If they are willing to capitalize on the chance, they can select projects that will increase their substantive knowledge and analytical and expressive skills.

Thus the choice a student makes will depend on his goals. For example, he may decide to focus on the operation of merely one of the many organizations dealing with the issue of pollution. This decision provides the focus for his research. Yet the choice is necessarily tentative. Let us explain why.

Whenever social research is described, the process is depicted as logical and rational. Steps are described in a precise order, as we have been doing here. Yet this description is an abstraction from reality: it tells how the steps logically relate, not how they actually occur in research. The parts of the research process are actually in constant interaction; they do not follow in a neat chronological sequence. The general topic and specific question chosen early in research are typically modified as the work progresses. The experienced analyst tries to capitalize on his discoveries rather than doggedly persist in a preplanned direction that proves disappointing. He may find that the access he expected fails to materialize, but he finds other good informants—people who are valuable sources of information—so he reshapes his specific question to highlight the promising sources. Thus his emphasis and focus may change. For example, he may start by asking, How much power do the poor have in this organization, but if the answer seems too obvious after initial proving, he can expand the question by asking, Why don't the poor have more power, or how has being in this organization affected them?

Many accounts of the actual development of projects have been written showing how the research sequence really occurred rather than how it logically should have progressed. For example, Selltiz and her associates describe how, because of limits on time, money, and the availability of appropriate evidence, compromises shaped a study of interracial relations (*Research Methods in Social Relations*, pp. 9–23). Remembering such reports, researchers accept the changes in their focus and activities that will inevitably occur.

TYPES OF TOPICS

So far, we have been describing a way of designing topics for empirical inquiry, assuming the student is expected to formulate his field work. However, there are many different types of field work topics. We shall describe some of them here because they may either help students design their topics or aid instructors who prefer to assign topics.

We distinguish four types of field work topics about which many different questions can be posed. Some topics deal with organizations or actual groups of people; others with segments of the population that do not form a real group; others with a policy issue or a process; and still others with a geographical area. Usually topics combine several of these dimensions; that is, a policy issue such as welfare is studied in respect to a particular organization, location, or segment of the population (the clients).

Organizations or groups to study may easily be found. Most people come into contact with many informal groups each day in living units, neighborhoods, jobs, and social and recreational activities. Lists of more formal groups such as churches, civic clubs, and governmental organizations are in community directories published by chambers of commerce and in telephone books. Telephone books cite political institutions by the name of the city, county, or state and also under the heading United States government. Addresses and telephone numbers of interesting accessible organizations are easy to compile from this source; telephone calls will provide information on activities and meeting times. The following list of political organizations shows the range of political field work experiences available in one metropolitan area (and thus is not inclusive for all areas):

CITY INSTITUTIONS

> City councils, mayors, and city managers
> Planning, police, and other commissions
> City attorney's offices and other departments
> Redevelopment agencies
> Poverty agencies
> Housing authorities
> Boards of education

COUNTY AND REGIONAL INSTITUTIONS

> Boards of supervisors
> County administrators

District attorneys
Public defenders
Courts (municipal and superior)
Welfare and other departments
Council of governments
Special districts, such as air pollution and rapid transit

STATE INSTITUTIONS

Departments such as Attorney General's Office, Human Resources, and Public Health
Water quality control board
Fair employment practices commission
Courts (Appeals and Supreme)
Local offices of state legislators (both houses)

FEDERAL INSTITUTIONS

Regional offices of such departments as Health, Education and Welfare, Housing and Urban Development, Labor, and Office of Economic Opportunity
Courts (Appeals and District)
Local offices of United States Senators and Representatives

PRIVATE GROUPS

Political parties
Labor unions
Voluntary associations, such as neighborhood improvement groups
Businesses

Examples of some of the important social science research on organizations or groups include:

PETER BLAU, *Dynamics of Bureaucracy*
MICHEL CROZIER, *The Bureaucratic Phenomenon*
ALVIN GOULDNER, *Patterns of Industrial Bureaucracy*
GEORGE HOMANS, *The Human Group*
SEYMOUR LIPSET and others, *Union Democracy*
PHILIP SELZNICK, *TVA and the Grass Roots*
JOHN WAHLKE and others, *The Legislative System*

A typical project studying a segment of the population is based on a survey. This technique requires a carefully designed questionnaire and sampling procedure to investigate old people, ghetto dwellers, socio-economic classes, and so on. Examples of this type of research include:

> GABRIEL ALMOND and SIDNEY VERBA, *The Civic Culture*
> ANGUS CAMPBELL and others, *The American Voter*
> AUGUST HOLLINGSHEAD and FREDERICK REDLICH, *Social Class and Mental Illness*

But there are other ways to study segments of the population. The structure of their lives can be observed in a carefully chosen field work setting. For example, old people can be studied in homes for the elderly or in trailer parks for retired people, as Sheila Johnson suggests in *Idle Haven;* affluent youths can be observed in high schools of wealthy communities. Topics dealing with segments of the population can be similar to topics concentrating on organizations if the field work setting involves interacting individuals, but the emphasis may differ. Some classic social science studies focusing on the lives and interactions of segments of the population are:

> HERBERT GANS, *The Urban Villagers*
> ERVING GOFFMAN, *Asylums*
> WILLIAM F. WHYTE, *Street Corner Society*

A third type of field work topic addresses policy issues or processes. This residual category is the broadest and the hardest to delineate. Yet these topics often come to mind in selecting research projects. The list of policy issues can be extended endlessly by simply following the mass media; they include questions about welfare, planning, civil rights, urban development, and so on. Whereas the topics previously discussed consider entities—organizations, categories, or individuals—issue topics typically involve many organizations and types of individuals. Such topics consider processes, interactions, and dynamics. Models for policy topics include:

> SCOTT GREER, *Urban Renewal and American Cities*
> ELIHU KATZ and PAUL LAZARSFELD, *Personal Influence*
> ANTHONY LEWIS, *Gideon's Trumpet*
> AARON WILDAVSKY, *The Politics of the Budgetary Process*

Geographical area topics comprise the fourth category; but often, area is combined with one of the preceding types of topics to help narrow this category. Organizations, populations, or policy issues will be studied in one town or subcommunity. Well-known community studies include:

ROBERT DAHL, *Who Governs*
FLOYD HUNTER, *Community Power Structure*
ARTHUR VIDICH and JOSEPH BENSMAN, *Small Town in a Mass Society*
W. LLOYD WARNER, ed., *Yankee City*

Some of the books previously mentioned, such as those by Gans and Whyte, have a strong geographical focus.

These four different types of topics show the diversity of subjects amenable to field work and the many different ways of approaching a general interest and thus narrowing a general topic into a worthwhile specific question. Suppose, for instance, a researcher is interested in desegregation. He may decide to ask how this issue affects a given organization or how that organization operates to affect desegregation policy; he may decide to look at people's attitudes or activities toward desegregation, or he may want to see how desegregation policies are formulated and administered at the national level or in various communities.

Each of the four types of topics can give rise to several different kinds of questions:

1. What are the important aspects of the issue being studied?
2. What are the causes of the issue being studied? (What independent variables account for the dependent variable?)
3. What are the consequences of the issue being studied? (What dependent variables follow from the independent variable?)
4. How could the issue being studied be changed?
5. What kinds of changes would have what results?

CONFIGURATION OF CLASS TOPICS

When an entire class is going to do field work, benefits can accrue from topic coordination, which may take several forms. If topics for individual projects are self-designed, people with similar projects can be placed in discussion groups after the topics are formulated (see the sample list of topics at the end of this chapter). Such groups allow for exchange of ideas about each project—ways to approach the topic, questions to ask, places to go and people to see for information, and methods for handling problems and evidence. Periodic discussions of field work are valuable because they allow students to think about their experiences, to relate the reality in which they are participating to intellectual frameworks. Discussion groups can also enable individuals who need interviews with the same person to make joint arrangements and thus minimize the demands on the respondent's time. These same groups can analyze completed work.

Self-designed topics also lend themselves to group projects. Individuals may decide to work together in formulating and researching a project. The finished product may be either coordinated, separate papers or one paper presenting a collection of all the work that the group members have done. Joint endeavors add numerous logistic and psychological complications to field work, but the opportunity for more ambitious research efforts and interactions make this type of coordination attractive to some researchers.

Field work coordination that involves either discussion groups or group projects is based on individual choice of projects. Some classes lend themselves to more structured forms of coordination whereby specific subdivisions of a central class topic are assigned to task forces. This class project approach means that component projects are cumulative rather than haphazard. One class, for example, studied the politics of a specific small city. With a geographical focus, the class members studied the political organizations and policies of that municipality. The central city task force looked at the council, mayor, manager, and commissions; another task force studied city departments and issues, including police, planning, and finance; another concentrated on city-based issues and organizations, such as waterfront development, schools, transportation, and redevelopment; and another studied county organizations located in the city, such as probation and health. Another group looked at regional issues and organizations, such as pollution; another studied state and federal programs in the city, such as welfare and manpower programs; and a final task force focused on citizens groups, such as the chamber of commerce, homeowners associations, and civil rights organizations.

Just as these types of topics may be combined in designing a question for research, the various forms of class coordination of topics may also be combined in numerous ways to produce different configurations of field work topics in one class. An assigned class topic and its subdivisions can still permit individuals to choose their component topic and decide whether they want to work in groups or individually. Assigned topics may be used without insisting on cumulative projects, as a way of decreasing the procrastination connected with self-designed projects. For example, one class divided a city into geographical areas (using neighborhoods or congressional districts as boundaries), assigning one student to each area. The task was to pick something within that area to study.

The resulting projects covered such topics as the opinions of retired people, the social impact of four churches, de facto segregation in one high school, the organization of a community movement, and life in an ethnic section of town.

GOOD QUESTIONS

Having described the formulation of topics, their variety, and possible configuration in a class, we now want to consider criteria for good researchable questions. These criteria are implicit in the previous discussion of choosing a specific question that is significant and interesting. They should be discussed even though evaluations of specific questions will obviously differ. What makes a question especially significant and interesting? What characteristics do the most interesting, significant questions have? What makes them outstanding? Excellent questions have the following characteristics:

They are *focused*—they take a particular aspect of a problem to allow an indepth treatment rather than a superficial synthesis of existing information. For example, What proposals are being made to reform education? A more focused question would be, What effect would open classroom proposals have on the output of educational systems?

They are *analytical*—they require probing inquiry rather than simple description or review of well-known background details. Probing means looking beneath the obvious to see (1) the actual phenomenon (including physical, intellectual, and emotional components), what is really going on, the informal patterns as well as the formal; (2) the connections between parts of the pattern and between one pattern and others; (3) why the phenomenon is occurring, the functions it is performing and its significance. For example, How does the board of education operate? A more analytical question is, Who dominates the board of education? or, What effect does the power structure of the board of education have on policy output? Another example would be, What is team teaching? Or, a more analytical question: How do student and teacher roles change in team teaching?

They are *provocatively stated*—they indicate why the topic is interesting and worth studying rather than simply blandly posing an exercise. For example, What is the occupational composition of teachers? A more provocative question would be, Are teachers predominantly middle class? If so, why, what effect does this finding have, and what could change the composition?

Now let us concentrate on the analytical aspects of good questions. One of the easiest pitfalls in field work is to rest content with anecdotes rather than with analysis. Sudden exposure to so many stimuli—telephone conversations, informal communications in halls and elevators, and tips from many sources—often overwhelms a field researcher. When he starts writing, he finds he can go on endlessly (in contrast to library papers where he may feel he has to "pad" his notes to meet length requirements). The problem is to use all the anecdotes to say something, to make a central point, to formulate or illuminate a hypothesis. And this thesis, or hypothesis, should be as analytical as possible. Take the pollution example used earlier in this chapter: If a field researcher decides to focus on the operation of only one of the antipollution groups, how could he frame an analytical question? Instead of asking how the group operates, which would enable him to stop at formal descriptions, he might ask how the group's operation compares with the formal description and why. Or he might ask how the group's behavior has been influenced by external pressure from private business, voluntary groups, or the national government. Or he might ask what mechanisms the organization uses to insulate itself from such pressures and the effect these mechanisms have on its antipollution activities.

Topics concerned with policies seem particularly conducive to description rather than analysis. Assessing the advantages and disadvantages of a policy reform, such as a voucher system for public education, by interviewing people to find out their positions, does not ordinarily make an excellent project. Just listing pros and cons does not go far enough. To be analytical, the researcher could ask what the real sources of the disagreement are, why the various proponents hold the views they do, what issues are not being raised that should be, or what evidence exists relevant to the issues raised.

Designing a field work project, as we have shown in this chapter, requires careful thought. General topics must be narrowed to specific questions, and a choice must be made among these questions on the basis of the availability of empirical evidence with educational and social value. The project can be done in groups or singly and should continuously be refined to be as probing as possible.

SAMPLE LIST OF FIELD WORK TOPICS

The following sample of self-selected topics was produced in one class in political science (the topics might just as easily have been in various other social sciences). Although they may fall short of the ideal criteria discussed in the text, these topics do show the abilities of students to generate a wide range of interesting projects. Students with similar topics were combined into discussion groups as described earlier in the chapter.

INTEREST GROUPS

What tactics are used by lobbyists to persuade legislators?

What role do lobbyists play in the state legislature?

How does the John Birch Society operate?

What is the relation of the state board of pharmacy to the pharmacists and to public health protection?

ELECTIONS AND PARTIES

In a nonpartisan election, how does the candidate organize his campaign to gain support from many segments of the community?

What roles did the local news media and businessmen's groups play in the mayoralty election?

What part do political parties actually play in nonpartisan local government?

How does a party headquarters function in the community?

POLITICS OF EDUCATION

How did the board of education reach its decision in the controversy over x?

Who dominates the board of education?

What forces have shaped the city's policy toward desegregating schools and allocating funds to minority schools?

What impact do the various teacher organizations have on local and state educational policy?

POLITICS OF HIGHER EDUCATION

How much do the people know about the university, and what do they think about the students and the value of education? (group project)

POLITICS OF WELFARE, POVERTY, URBAN RENEWAL, AND HOUSING

What forces influenced the urban renewal project?

How effective has the state department of human resources been?

How well coordinated are the various poverty programs?

How much conflict exists between state and local levels over the control of welfare programs?

What might be done to improve the administration of emergency medical care?

POLITICS OF RACE

What influence does black nationalism have on city policy?

How do minority groups mobilize to try to gain political power?

What has the city government done to improve conditions in ethnic ghettos?

POLITICS OF TRANSPORTATION

What are the economic and political constraints on the development of rapid transit in this city?

What tactics are being used by groups favoring rapid transit?

Can groups in this community be successful in preventing construction of a new expressway?

POLITICS OF POLLUTION

How much influence are antismog groups able to exert?

What strategies did groups use to force a referendum on a power generating plant?

How is the city handling the problem of refuse disposal pollution?

What forces have influenced the policy on offshore drilling?

What is the regional water quality control board doing about water pollution?

POLITICS OF LAW ENFORCEMENT

How do law enforcement officers view themselves, society, and their role in society?

What influence has the rise of protest had on police policy and practice?

What is the political significance of the prosecutor in state courts?

In what ways can the district attorney influence public policy?

How effective are public defenders?

How does the National Guard fulfill its role in law enforcement?

POLITICS OF CITY AND COUNTY GOVERNMENT

To what extent does local government constrain the suburban business sector?

How does the city council reach decisions?

How do federal and state grants influence local government?

How effective are the advisory commissions to the county governing board?

Would a strong mayor be more responsive to the community?

methods of field work

3

In choosing a question, the field researcher should consider the availability of empirical evidence; but once he decides on the question, he should concentrate on collecting data. No matter how skillfully he has designed the research problem, the project will not fulfill its promise unless the field work is productive.

VALUES, EVIDENCE, AND SOCIAL SCIENCE ETHICS

Social scientists do not believe that facts speak for themselves. They know that the personal values of the researcher enter into every phase of his work—selection of a topic and of methods, perception of evidence, interpretation of evidence, and use made of results. (For further discussion of this point, see Abraham Kaplan, *The Conduct of Inquiry,* pp. 370–410.) The presence of a researcher may change the setting he is trying to study. Yet empirical evidence is not infinitely malleable; facts are not simply the values of the researcher. In research the evidence should not be shaped to fit the analyst's predispositions. He must respect the independent existence of the evidence. If evidence is totally manipulated by the researcher, then the research is an illusion.

The social scientist knows well the resistance of data, the obstinate way they at times refuse to fit the investigator's pre-existing values and hypotheses. Starting off expecting to find *x*, he finds something that is not *x*, and he cannot make the discovery fit the expectation by checking for errors, recollecting data, or reinterpreting evidence. This tension between ideas and evidence can exist even though he only knows the evidence through his perceptual screens. The contradiction is a source of both excitement and pain of field work, as ideas are challenged by the evidence and as the professional ethics of the researcher are tested. Is he willing to manipulate the data to eliminate the tension between the evidence and his ideas? Is he willing to misuse the evidence so that he will not challenge his preconceptions or those of his peers or his sponsors? Or is he willing to modify the evidence to support provocative statements he desires to make despite contradictory evidence?

Social science ethics oblige the researcher to report evidence as accurately as possible. He must not attempt to manipulate data to fit his preconceptions. The analyst attempts to be self-conscious about his values, knowing how they shape the field work and compensating for this influence as much as possible. The goal of field work is to use evidence to give as accurate a picture as possible, which other social scientists would recognize as fair (because it adheres to rules for use of evidence) even though they might not accept it as adequate.

We use the term *accurate* rather than *objective* because objective is sometimes understood to mean value free, and we have already indicated that research is not value free. But neither is it simply a mechanism for supporting one's biases, for indulging in advocacy, or giving rhetoric a gloss of scientific respectability. Later, in talking about uses of research, we shall indicate that the use of research results is not neutral, but here we insist that a social scientist should attempt to be neutral in gathering evidence. He must relate what he sees as he sees it and not as he wishes he saw it. If he cannot "see" evidence unless it fits his wishes, he should not attempt to do research. True research involves the willingness to modify one's assumptions in light of the evidence.

FOUR METHODS

What then are the methods of obtaining empirical evidence and of making research productive? Many texts are devoted to the consideration of social science methods, such as:

> LEON FESTINGER and DANIEL KATZ, *Research Methods in the Behavioral Sciences*
> WILLIAM GOODE and PAUL HATT, *Methods in Social Research*
> JOHN MADGE, *The Tools of Social Science*

This book considers only methods applicable to field work. The primary ones are:

1. observation or participant observation
2. interviews
3. questionnaires
4. analysis of available records

This chapter briefly describes field work methods and their strengths and weaknesses; the next chapter considers how to use these methods. We are not interested in their intricacies but in conveying sufficient information about them so that people can use them in the field for worthwhile projects. Sophistication in the methods is more appropriate after firsthand experience has been gained rather than before. People who have done empirical research often become highly motivated to improve their techniques, and they thus benefit from courses in detailed methodology. Such courses are less valuable for students to whom research is merely an abstract exercise.

OBSERVATION

Observation is a basic method in the social sciences. It involves watching what is going on, who is doing what to whom, where, when, and how. Social science observation differs from the everyday observations everybody makes by being more systematic. The social scientist analyzes occurrences he observes to find patterns and to link them with organizing concepts and theories so that more general conclusions can be drawn about the patterns. For example, he looks to see how handling a controversy at a city council meeting illustrates more general propositions about the relation of the controversy to the political system. Behind the observation are always the questions, what does this illustrate, what is it a case of, what is its significance? Such analysis requires more precise observations than people ordinarily make. For example, it is not enough to come away from the city council meeting with the report that the controversy resulted in much shouting but nothing happened. The next chapter suggests ways of making more systematic observation.

Observation is an invaluable method for discovering actual behavior. Participants' descriptions of behavior may differ widely from what actually occurred because much happens that participants are not aware of or do not want to discuss.

Observation has shortcomings, however. It does not reveal why the behavior occurs or what people's attitudes are about it. The analyst's observations are also subject to the limitations of his perceptions. Just as participants' reports of what happens will differ, so will researchers' perceptions vary. Observation also requires a great deal of time because behavior in which the researcher is interested often takes place at unpredictable times, so he ends up watching much extraneous activity. Further, observation is not always possible. Certain activities may be inaccessible even to the most ingenious researcher.

Examples of studies using observation for collecting data are:

OSCAR LEWIS, *The Children of Sanchez*
ELLIOT LIEBOW, *Tally's Corner*
SAMUEL WALLACE, *Skid Row as a Way of Life*

PARTICIPANT OBSERVATION

An important variation of observation is called participant observation: the researcher becomes a member of the activity he is observing. A continuum of observation methods may be constructed, which varies according to the involvement of the researcher, from none to complete involvement. No agreement exists on how much participation is essential for the participant observation method, so no rigid distinction between observation and participant observation will be made here. However, participant observation implies an immersion in the activity being studied and an attempt to see the world the way the subjects see it.

Participant observation provides a closer look at behavior than observation does. The researcher can ask all kinds of casual questions as events occur because he is known in the group. For example, he can ask, Why did everyone laugh at what was just said? He will pick up many leads from informal asides that people make at lunch or while they walk down halls. The disadvantages of observation also apply to participant observation, and the problems of accuracy are heightened by the length and depth of the investigator's involvement. As Jacqueline Wiseman and Marcia Aron have pointed out, like an espionage agent, a participant observer must function simultaneously in two frames of reference: he is an insider who must still maintain his ability to see the phenomena from the outside, and he must constantly guard against both aversion and overidentification.

INTERVIEWS

The interview is a second essential field work method. People associated with a topic being studied are personally questioned about their opinions. An interview, after ascertaining a respondent's socioeconomic characteristics, can focus on his knowledge, feelings, and perceptions of other people's opinions and behavior. An interview, according to Claire Selltiz and her associates, may provide information about "what a person knows, believes or expects, feels or wants, intends or does or has done, and about his explanations or reasons for any of the preceding" (*Research Methods in Social Relations*, p. 243).

Because interviews can provide such information, they have strengths observation does not have. But their shortcomings are the opposite of observation. An interview cannot tell what is actually happening; people may not want to be frank, or they may not actually know their real interests and feelings. Like observation, interviewing is influenced by the biases of the researcher—how he asks the questions and which people he chooses to interview.

The format of interviews varies from totally structured to unstructured. Structured interviews are also called standardized interviews. Questions are given in the same order with the same wording to every respondent. The questions typically have fixed alternative responses such as strongly agree, agree, disagree, strongly disagree, but they may also be open-ended, such as What do you see as the main problems in this agency? Unstructured interviews—also called focused, depth, or nondirective—vary the questions to fit the characteristics of the respondent and the purpose of each interview. For instance, an interviewer might not want to ask a judge the same questions about judicial reform as he would ask a defendant or a prosecuting attorney. In unstructured interviews the exact questions and the wording of questions are not predetermined.

Flexibility is the obvious advantage of unstructured interviews. An interviewer can make observations about the setting and the feelings of the respondents, and he can adjust approaches to reach best the goals of the interview. For example, he can sense whether a respondent is being reticent and can encourage the respondent to relax and be frank; he can probe when the person suspects that feelings are being suppressed out of politeness.

But unstructured interviewing, like observations, can be time consuming. Because respondents often want to tell much more than is needed for a project, the interviewer may sit through several hours of conversation for only a few minutes' worth of data. In addition the problem of analyzing noncomparable answers can be staggering. Yet unstructured interviews are particularly helpful for exploratory studies in which so little is known about a subject that structured questions would be premature, forcing subjects to give misleading responses. Unstructured interviews can reveal significant factors and relationships that would not have occurred to the investigator.

Examples of studies using interviews are:

JOHN BOLLENS, ed., *Exploring the Metropolitan Community*
MORTON DEUTSCH and MARY COLLINS, *Interracial Housing*
KENNETH KENISTON, *Young Radicals*
ROBERT LANE, *Political Ideology*
JAMES WILSON, *Negro Politics*

Although many studies rely on only one of the two methods described so far, the two actually complement each other. Activities that seem incomprehensible to an observer may have meaning when a participant is interviewed and explains his perspective on what was happening. Similarly the opportunity to observe respondents in action can be an important aid in assessing their interview responses.

QUESTIONNAIRES

The questionnaire method, a variation of the interview technique, is a written form of a structured interview. Instead of sending interviewers into the field asking questions, this method calls for sending or handing questionnaires to respondents who are asked to write down their responses and return the forms.

Either questionnaires or structured interviews are used to do surveys. Surveys are designed to gather information from a representative sample of a population, which is generalized to a whole population. The survey technique is well known to the public familiar with various professional political and consumer attitudinal polling organizations. Many social science departments offer methodology courses emphasizing survey research with respect to both collection and analysis of data. But major surveys are ambitious and costly undertakings, requiring large numbers of trained interviewers and analysts plus data processing equipment. Thus full-fledged surveys are typically executed by private organizations or university-related survey research centers, such as the National Opinion Research Center of the University of Chicago and the survey research centers at the University of Michigan and the University of California, Berkeley.

Cooperative agreements between survey organizations make data accumulated for one study available for secondary analysis by other researchers to see what the data show about other topics. For example, in *The Civic Culture*, Gabriel Almond and Sydney Verba surveyed 1,000 people in each of five countries to compare cross-national attitudes toward political systems. But the responses from the United States may be studied to compare the political efficacy of black and white Americans.

Although secondary analysis is useful, it does not enable students to do field work; therefore it will not be discussed further in this book. And because the survey method and the problems of selecting a representative sample are discussed so fully in the literature and require many resources, they will not be emphasized here.

Some students, however, may want to use questionnaires or structured interviews as their field work method. For example, students are often interested in studying the attitudes toward students of residents in a college community. If a small group of students is willing to work together on such a project, the students should be able to get a sufficient number of responses to discover some interesting patterns even without the help of computers or sophisticated sampling techniques. Nevertheless, they must be aware of the limitations of their evidence.

The advantages of questionnaires or structured interviews are the quantifiability and the comparability of the results. Substantial amounts of information about large numbers of people can be collected and analyzed relatively easily. Especially when questionnaires are distributed by mail, respondents are assured of anonymity and are able to take more time to consider their answers. These strengths also entail weaknesses. The information obtained may be superficial or misleading. Structured queries limit the types of possible responses. Many important nuances may be lost, and information about dynamics and contexts is often lost. Mail questionnaires are also notoriously difficult to collect. Response rates differ widely depending on the population being studied; a return rate of only 50 percent is not considered at all unusual, and to get even that many questionnaires returned may take a long time. For more on questionnaires and surveys, see:

CHARLES BACKSTROM and GERALD HURSH, *Survey Research*
HERBERT HYMAN, *Survey Design and Analysis*
HARRY SCOBLE and STANLEY BACHRACK, "Mailed Questionnaires: Controlled Reduction of Nonresponse"
EVE WEINBERG, *Community Surveys with Local Talent*

Examples of studies using questionnaires include:

ALFRED KINSEY and others, *Sexual Behavior in the Human Male*
HARRY SCOBLE, *Ideology and Electoral Action*

ANALYSIS OF AVAILABLE RECORDS

At first, the final method of gathering data—analysis of available records—might seem to involve simply library work and thus not to be appropriate to a discussion of field work. Certainly a great many kinds of records are available in large libraries. Compilations of quantitative data, called aggregate data to distinguish it from survey data about individuals, can be useful. For example, aggregate data can give a profile of the residents of an area—average age, income, education, and so forth. However, many kinds of written records are not generally available in libraries. Minutes of an organization's meetings, annual reports, the results of citizen task forces and special studies, and correspondence may only be kept at the organization's offices. Similarly back issues of local newspapers may only be available in the newspapers' offices, and newspapers maintain libraries of clippings from their papers arranged by topics.

Analysis of available records is rarely used as the sole method of field research, but it is almost always employed to supplement the other, previously discussed methods.

CHOICE OF METHODS

Having become familiar with the strengths and weaknesses of the different methods for gathering empirical evidence, the researcher should be ready to select the methods best fitted to the problem he has chosen for investigation. The techniques he selects should give the most accurate and pertinent information on the topic. Ingenuity is a crucial trait at this stage. He might ask, What is it I want to know? What methods will give me the information I need?

Typically the decision is made to combine several methods because the strengths and shortcomings can compensate for each other. Diversity gives helpful multiple fixes on a problem. Thus unstructured interviews with selected planners in a given city can supplement questionnaire results from a wider spectrum of planners. Another way to increase the accuracy and significance of field work is to design comparative research. For example, in investigating city planning, the researcher might gather evidence on city planners in more than one city or in various organizations within one city so that it will be easier to see what accounts for specific findings. Do they occur in diverse settings, or are they simply the result of circumstances unique to one setting?

Then, when developing the details of the methods he chooses, the researcher continually asks, What will doing that tell me? Will it give me the material I need to deal with my topic? Such questions are necessary antidotes to the tendency to proliferate minutiae of methods and forget one's focus. For instance, when developing a plan of what to ask interviewees, the researcher may be tempted to keep adding interesting questions. Eventually he throws in so many items that the interview gets out of hand—too lengthy and rambling, a general fishing expedition. Occasionally such interviews can be enjoyable and enlightening, but the day of reckoning comes when the interviewer sits down to analyze the response and discovers that "nothing adds up." He has numerous tidbits on a wide variety of issues but not enough on any one item to reveal patterns.

Just as the last chapter stressed the importance of narrowing topics, this one stresses the importance of using methods appropriate to topics. One way of checking whether these steps have been followed is the writing of a research design.

RESEARCH DESIGN

A research design describes as concisely as possible the plan the researcher has decided on. Such a design should be written before he starts to do field work because it encourages clarity. Later modifications are inevitable and desirable, but it is useful to have a plan to deviate from rather than to flounder around continuously, waiting for some perfect scheme to reveal itself. A research design typically includes discussion of:

1. purpose
2. problem to be investigated
3. specific setting and subjects to be studied (for example, the organization and the people within that organization)
4. methods of gathering evidence
5. content of interviews, questionnaires, and observations
6. analysis of data

A tentative work schedule may also be useful.

The selection of a specific research question and appropriate methods of gathering empirical evidence results in a research design. But so far the research has involved planning rather than participation—much more planning than some might expect. Yet this essential aspect of systematic field work helps ensure that the next stage of the work will be worthwhile.

how to do work
in the field

4

Once a topic and the methods of research have been chosen, the field work stage of the project begins. This chapter concentrates on how to do field work and discussses routines that researchers ordinarily do not make explicit. After doing field work, each person develops his particular style and feel for the complexities in the process. Attempting to convey field work skills to others involves the same frustrations as trying to teach how to write, paint, or teach. These activities require much more than a mechanical repetition of transferable skills.

Our discussion of field work suggestions does not pretend to be comprehensive or sufficient to turn someone into a seasoned researcher. Our purpose is to provide a guide so that a person feels sufficiently confident to try field work. We feel certain that once under way he will discover many other techniques that work well for him. The danger of making any field work procedures explicit is that they may unintentionally make field work sound difficult. We have all had the experience of reading directions for some habitual activity (tying shoes, for example) and finding that self-conscious attention to the process makes it sound much more complicated than it actually is. Thus the reader should look in this chapter for ideas *he* can use. His work should soon demonstrate better than any words can that field work techniques come naturally once they are tried.

Discussion of the field work process is approximately chronological, but the reader should remember that such order is deceptive since events are not orderly and flexibility is essential to productive research. Researchers learn to adjust their plans to unexpected occurrences. For example, if air pollution regulations that are being studied are suddenly revised, changes in the research design and time schedule are inevitable. Furthermore, field work varies according to the problem under consideration and the methods in use. Not all suggestions made here will be appropriate to every specific project. If the reader is not observing any meetings, for example, the guides to observation will not be useful. Yet we have placed all the procedural discussions in one chapter rather than separated them according to methods because the pattern of empirical inquiry has many similarities regardless of the methods involved.

HYPOTHESES

As he selects his question and methods, the researcher should also be speculating about the results he may obtain. What types of answers to the question seem possible? What does he expect to find out? Such reflection usually leads to hunches or hypotheses about what he might find. These hypotheses are important in shaping the research. They help indicate what he should be looking for, what types of evidence may be important. Thus an essential step in the field work stage is the development of working hypotheses that will be supported or challenged by the empirical findings.

A closely related step is operationalizing concepts—that is, deciding what empirical evidence will be accepted as an indicator of each concept under investigation. For example, if a researcher's hypothesis is that the larger the organization the less responsive it is to changes in its environment, what actions will he accept as indicators of changes in organizations—total transformation in its structure, rewording of a regulation, or both? Such working definitions are essential to empirical research because they provide standards for interpreting data. Without operational definitions the researcher does not know what the empirical evidence means, what answers it gives. Yet operationalizing is one of the most difficult aspects of a research project. At best the indicators can only be limited reflections of the underlying concept; at worst they can completely distort the significance of evidence. Thus decisions about what indicators to use are important and difficult.

BACKGROUND READING

Considerable knowledge about the topic helps greatly in formulating hypotheses and carrying out field work. Background reading can often help the researcher to formulate a sharper, more interesting question, better hypotheses, and more incisive field work. For instance, the more the researcher knows before he conducts an interview with the director of an urban renewal agency, the better chance he has of getting beyond the elementary facts. If he is unprepared for such an interview he runs the risk of having the session wasted on information easily available in public relations brochures.

Background reading may also reveal studies that can serve as models for field work. For example, if the researcher were interested in studying the relations among various governmental programs in a specific locality, James Sundquist's *Making Federalism Work* might be a good starting point. It cites relevant literature and makes generalizations that could be hypotheses for further studies. The themes in the book also provide ties to further ideas, which will have a great deal more significance when linked with existing bodies of knowledge.

Often instructors will suggest specific background reading. But let us review briefly some of the standard sources of social science information other than books.

Library reference rooms contain social science bibliographies and encyclopedias that provide guides to literature on specific topics. Such sources are usually better starting places than library card catalogs because the reference works furnish an overview of literature in a given field. General reference works include:

BERT HOSELITZ, ed., *A Reader's Guide to the Social Sciences*
DAVID SILLS, ed., *International Encyclopedia of the Social Sciences*
CARL WHITE and associates, *Sources of Information in the Social Sciences*

Many specialized bibliographies are also available in reference rooms. For example:

BARBARA HUDSON and ROBERT MCDONALD, *Metropolitan Communities, A Bibliography Supplement: 1958–1964*

Journals usually have more timely material than books. Library reference rooms have indexes to periodicals such as:

Social Sciences and Humanities Index (formerly *International Index to Periodicals*)—index of scholarly journals
Public Affairs Information Service Bulletin—index of periodical articles, pamphlets, government documents and books relating to economic and social conditions, public administration, and international affairs
Reader's Guide to Periodical Literature—index of many popular journals.

Since articles in such journals are rarely sufficient for research background, students are urged to look beyond the necessarily general information in such magazines for more sophisticated, analytical material.

Libraries typically have a newspaper collection composed of major local newspapers and some out-of-city papers. The following newspapers have indexes: *New York Times, Wall Street Journal,* and *Christian Science Monitor.*

Some libraries have special collections of national, state, and local government publications. Many large libraries are depositories of federal documents; that is, they are regularly sent a wide selection of national government publications. Libraries not designated as depositories often have a number of federal documents. Federal, state, and local government publications are valuable resources too often overlooked. They provide current information on many interesting topics. Legislative committees, executive departments, and special commissions publish reports about numerous organizations, problems, segments of the population, and geographical areas of the nation. Prominent examples are the report of the National Advisory Commission on Civil Disorders (Kerner Commission), the supplementary studies done for the Commission, and the various reports prepared by the President's Commission on Law Enforcement and the Administration of Justice.

Federal publications are listed in the *Monthly Catalogue of United States Government Publications,* which has an annual index. Other useful sources of general background information on the national government are: *United States Government Organization Manual,* which describes the agencies of the legislative, judicial, and executive branches; and the *Congressional Quarterly* and the *National Journal,* private publications that summarize current government activities.

States list their publications under various titles. For instance, the California list is called *California State Publications.* Some libraries have the *Monthly Checklist of State Publications,* which shows items from all states that are received by the U. S. Library of Congress.

No standard indexes of local government publications exist, but any government documents library can provide information on what material it has available. A useful guide to standard sources on local communities is E. E. Schattschneider and Victor Jones, *Local Political Surveys.*

Large libraries may have special collections of interest for particular topics. Universities typically have special institutes or bureaus that have library collections. For example, they may have institute libraries that have monographs and pamphlets on government, economic, or social research concerning public issues, often primarily state and local which are generally not available elsewhere.

More information on the social sciences is presented in:

RALPH ANDREANO and others, *The Student Economist's Handbook*

PAULINE BART and LINDA FRANKEL. *The Student Sociologist Handbook*

RICHARD MERRITT and GLORIA PYSKA, *The Student Political Scientist's Handbook*

THEODORE SARBIN and WILLIAM COLE, *The Student Psychologist's Handbook*

ELABORATING RESEARCH DESIGN

After doing background reading and formulating hypotheses, the researcher plans the details of his field work. He elaborates on his research design, deciding where he will go, what he will do when he gets there, and what he will watch for or ask about. These detailed plans will change frequently as some avenues turn out to be unproductive and as unexpected opportunities appear.

There are many different strategies for deciding what to observe or whom to interview. The researcher might ask advice from people familiar with the topic and compile in advance a list of their suggestions. He might then select from this list the combination of activities that will give him maximum diversity.

The researcher should try to obtain a wide variety of views on a topic. For example, in studying the image of a police department, he might decide to talk with senior members of the department, new recruits, people arrested by the department, and members of various socioeconomic groups in the community. Or in studying the operation of a comprehensive health planning council, he might look at a general council meeting, an executive council session, and several different committee meetings as well as the followup activities of the staff and various council members. Research that relies heavily on only one type of viewpoint is shallow and unconvincing. For example, a conclusion that a teen club is meeting the needs of its members solely on the basis of interviews with the staff is unacceptable.

Another strategy for selecting respondents is called the snowball technique. The researcher gets just enough advice to decide where to start and then collects suggestions about whom else to interview or what else to observe from each contact he makes. This technique puts the researcher in the field rapidly, but he is less certain of obtaining diverse evidence. Often a combination of the two techniques works well, selecting from a tentative list of possibilities and then, while the field work is under way, asking respondents to suggest other alternatives. Thus the researcher's plan is purposely left flexible.

The order in which the researcher carries out his observations and interviews can also be important. Should he go first to what he suspects will be his best sources? We prefer to go to such sources early in the field work but not first. We choose to go to easy sources initially, where our chances of success are best, so we can become familiar with the issues involved, with the types of responses our questions may elicit, or the kinds of behavior we may observe. This is really part of the pretesting of any research project and, when questionnaires are involved, such a pretest is an essential part of the process. We recommend pretesting any plan, by trying it out in situations where a failure will not be a disaster. For instance, if a project hinges on determining the actions of a key figure, such as a director of an organization, and the researcher talks with this key person before being sure of himself and his information, he may be thwarted and have worn out his welcome, thus making a return visit impossible.

Often the researcher should arrange his field work so that he is exposed alternately to contrasting views. This juxtaposition can alert him to important issues that he would not have seen if he had only heard one point of view during a segment of his work.

GETTING STARTED ON FIELD CONTACT

Despite the importance of planning field work, it is equally important not to overplan. Lengthy procrastination about research designs may bring the law of diminishing returns into operation. A researcher may worry so much about the possibility of problems that he never gets the stimulus that comes from contact with other people also interested in his topic. Many problems are easily resolved once the field work is under way, partly because of the increased motivation field work typically provides. Yet vacillation and procrastination are common reactions to the immediate prospect of coming into direct contact with new people and situations. Even some seasoned researchers feel nervous before each initial contact.

"Tricks of the trade" may help the researcher overcome such obstacles. Rather than be deterred by failure, he should keep trying. Although refusals or interviews and observations that prove nonproductive are discouraging, these experiences are an inevitable part of most field work. Experienced researchers are fortified during such moments by the knowledge that breakthroughs can also be expected. They know that negative results can be as revealing as positive ones, showing what is not possible and indicating interesting patterns. For example, the researcher can easily leave a hearing of a visiting national or state legislative committee in disgust because "nothing is going on"; yet he might ask, Why isn't anything going on and what does that suggest about the operation of this committee? After interviewing many judges and getting what he perceived as evasive answers, one student wrote an insightful paper on "why you can't ever get a straight answer from a judge." He developed this theme by showing the diverse constraints operating on judges and the pattern of their reactions to these constraints.

ACCESS

In many types of research, gaining access to sources of information is easy. The researcher merely goes to public places, whether street corners or public meetings, and watches what is going on. He does not need anybody's approval and nobody will wonder what he is doing.

But for other research projects access may be more difficult. If the researcher wants to observe private activities, such as staff meetings of an organization, or to talk with specific people, willing subjects are essential.

The easiest way to get access to a group is to be part of that group already. Many jobs, intern programs, and volunteer activities provide easy access opportunities for students. As participant observers they may increase the value of their experience by systematically studying the operation of the group to which they belong. For example, an intern in a private organization such as Common Cause should be able to obtain and conduct revealing interviews with its leaders if he is interested in capitalizing on such research opportunities. Many campuses have offices that serve as central sources of information on opportunities for students to participate in community activities. Community groups call such offices and describe the kind of help they need.

If access is not automatic, what can be done? When time is ample, students can offer their services to organizations. They can do a wide variety of volunteer tasks, such as writing proposals or conducting needed research. Thus they gain access to a group by doing something for it, and then, after demonstrating their interest, they can proceed with research. Certain organizations such as public schools have policies that strictly limit research access to protect their members from constant intrusions. However, once he is known and trusted by the members, the researcher will find that he can conduct his research without exploiting the rapport he has built. Some community groups have been plagued by so many researchers that they resent interviewers who study the group without doing anything for it. In such cases access will require time for contributing to the organization as well as for studying it. When students do volunteer work for organizations as part of a field project, they should make clear the conditions they set on the work they are doing. For instance, they should specify what they expect to get in return for the work, such as a chance to attend certain meetings.

When time is short, direct requests to observe or interview are necessary. The researcher should ask to interview or observe the person in the organization he thinks most likely to approve. If the person agrees, he may be willing to help the researcher make further arrangements. A letter of introduction may be helpful but usually is unnecessary.

In your role as the researcher, remember, in deciding on the individual to contact initially, to use any personal leads you have, such as the friend of a friend. Mention the name of the mutual friend when calling for appointments. Or ask people familiar with your topic for suggestions about whom to see at first. If your need is general background, a talk with a public relations officer is sufficient; but if you want to find out the official position of an organization, try to speak to the highest level person knowledgeable about the topic. If you do not know such a person's name, call and ask for the chief executive's office. The title of the chief executive varies: president (particularly in private community and business organizations), executive director (in both private and public activities), governor, mayor, and chairman are the most frequent. Explain your project to the executive's personal secretary, saying you would like to know which deputies or department heads would be most familiar with the topic. Then when you follow up on this lead, you can tell this individual's secretary that the chief executive's secretary suggested that you talk with this office. If a secretary says X is too busy, ask who else might be able to help you. If you have trouble getting an appointment over the telephone, go to the office to make one personally.

When you complete an interview, ask the respondent whom else you should interview; and when you call for that appointment, mention who gave you the new subject's name. If you have interviewed people opposed to a certain position, but the people in favor are reluctant to be interviewed, explain that you have already interviewed an opponent and would like to hear the other side of the issue. It is often easy to gain access to former members of an organization in which you are interested. Too often overlooked, they can be valuable sources of information with unique perspectives and the freedom to be candid.

When making interview appointments, explain that you are doing research for a class and will keep sources anonymous if they so desire. If the research is part of your career interest, mention this fact to show your serious concern with the topic. If several class members want to interview the same person or observe the same meeting, they should make the arrangements together so they make the least possible demands on the subject's time. If ten members of a class request separate appointments with the same public figure, they will undoubtedly feel repercussions that might jeopardize future field work. But if those same ten students coordinate their efforts, reception to their request should improve markedly.

Students have often found that obtaining interviews is not nearly as hard as they had expected. Tales of research experiences are endless: one researcher called the chairman of a state regulatory commission fully expecting to have the interview request rejected and instead was told to come in the next day. Another researcher was invited to lunch by a respondent. Still another researcher was "kicked upstairs" to higher and higher officers in an organization because no one wanted to take the responsibility of speaking on a controversial topic. Of course, there are other stories of unanswered telephone calls and letters, and repeated reports that X is at a meeting and the secretary has no idea when he can be reached. Researchers who depend on getting instant data are unrealistic. But if they allow enough time, pleasant persistence usually achieves good results.

Social scientists do not agree on whether it is proper for researchers to conceal their research activities from the subjects. Many social scientists prefer to do research where they can tell their subjects in a general way what they are doing. However, researchers must be careful not to give so many details that the respondents will attempt to manipulate answers to influence outcomes. People who tell subjects they are doing research are often surprised at how helpful the subjects will be, perhaps remembering people who aided them with past tasks or perhaps simply glad to have someone interested in them.

CONDUCTING INTERVIEWS

Interview styles differ considerably. Each interviewer gradually finds the style that best fits his personality and purpose. But consider these general suggestions.

The more you know before the interview, the more probing the interview can be. In addition to background reading, find out as much as possible about the person you intend to interview. How long has he been in his present position? What kind of training has he had? What other things has he done? What are his socioeconomic and educational characteristics? Sometimes friends, fellow workers, or secretaries can give this kind of information (secretaries often will give out a copy of their employer's résumé, describing aspects of his career and some personal characteristics).

Questions to ask

Before the interview, plan the topics you wish to cover and the questions you will use. An interview may have open-ended questions such as, What do you think about the other members of this group? What do you think about X? What is happening here? An interview may also consist of structured questions, which are read in exactly the same way to each respondent who must select an answer from the choices provided. No variations are permitted. Examples of structured interview questions can be found in the appendixes of many social science studies, such as Angus Campbell and associates' *The American Voter,* Gabriel Almond and Sydney Verba's *The Civic Culture,* and Elihu Katz and Paul Lazarsfeld's *Personal Influence.* Become familiar with the standard questions used in such studies to measure efficacy, partisanship, militancy, and other attitudes.

As you plan your questions, consider the following:

1. Do the questions provide the researcher with the information needed to answer the problem being studied?
2. Are the respondents able and willing to answer?
3. Are the questions objective? (A biased question indicates to the respondent what a "proper" answer is; for example, You don't agree with our policy in federal aid to education, do you?)
4. Are the questions clear?

The best way to see whether your questions meet these criteria is to pretest them. Try out your interview plan on several different people to find problems you failed to spot.

The list of possible interview questions is endless. For example, consider the following sample questions, which could be used in talking with members of an organization to find out how the organization operates. Notice, however, that the interviewer must select the items central to his topic. We have already stressed the importance of designing a focused topic. Such a topic then allows the researcher to *choose pertinent questions.* Thus although the following questions are appropriate to the general issue of organizational operation, this topic formulation is much too broad for an actual research project.

ORGANIZATION'S GOALS

What are your organization's stated goals? Its actual goals?
What are the goals of your office? Of other offices in the organization?

How are the various goals determined?
How are conflicts between various goals handled?
What problems might be involved if you were to change the goals?

INDIVIDUAL'S ROLES

What kind of work do you do?
How do you conceive your job?
What do others expect of you?
Who is important to you in your job?
What conflicts exist between your goals and the organization's goals?
What kinds of contact do you have with people in other offices?

CALCULATIONS AND STRATEGIES

What problems do you encounter in your job?
How do you make decisions about what to do?
How far ahead do you plan?
How do you go about getting what you ask for?
Are certain people in your office more influential than others?

CLIENTELE RELATIONS

What people outside the organization are interested in its activities?
How much influence do they have on the operation of the organization?
How is the influence exerted?
Do you have contact with the clientele?

Beginning the Interview

Most interviewers start a session by briefly reviewing their research and offering assurances that responses will be anonymous. For example, "When I made the appointment, I explained that I'm doing a study of how this organization makes policy decisions. I'm trying to get the opinions of as many department heads as possible, and I promise that the sources of my information won't be revealed." The usual pattern is to start with easy questions, which get the respondent talking on a familiar subject. For instance, "Could you tell me what your job involves?" Then as you build rapport and trust, the interview can go on to more difficult or personal questions.

Overly aggressive interviewers, who act as if they know all the answers and intend to grill the respondent to prove to him the error of his ways, can ruin an interview. Such an opening puts the subject on the defensive and may unintentionally reveal the interviewer's naïveté. He may later be embarrassed to find out that he could have learned something from the subject after all.

Guiding an Unstructured Interview

An essential skill in unstructured interviewing is probing, following promising leads in the conversation and getting the respondents to elaborate on these points. (In interview notes, responses elicited by probes are preceded by slash marks such as /). Some ways of probing are: Tell me more about that. How do you explain that? How do you feel about that?

There are many ways of attempting to get more than surface responses. Convey the impression that you are well informed on the subject so the respondent does not need to review the elementary facts. Stress that you are interested in finding out what is actually going on, the behind-the-scenes information—"I'd appreciate your really leveling with me on this." Bring up other opinions on an issue, which may conflict with the respondent's views, and ask him how he accounts for the differences.

An abrasive style works well for some researchers, who feel that by challenging respondents with difficult issues, the respondents will answer more spontaneously and not give superficial replies. However, this approach may make a respondent angry rather than open and may preclude further contact with him. Because interviewers must convey the impression that they are open-minded and are striving to be fair about all aspects of a topic, any challenges they do pose should usually be done in the third person. For example, "Many people have told me that they do not support the view you have just expressed." The safest style is to be open and understanding, avoiding taking sides.

A common problem in unstructured interviews is for researchers to talk too much. They start giving their views, forgetting that the purpose of the interview is to discover another person's opinions. In general you should say no more than is necessary to make the respondent feel at ease and to keep him talking freely. Often a nod of the head or a "yes, I know" is sufficient.

Another, less serious but troublesome problem is to find a tactful way of cutting off an answer that is getting too far off the subject. For example, you might say, "I'd like to raise a different point" or "I know your time is short, and I want to be sure to cover a few more things." Before ending the interview, you might say that you would like to telephone the respondent if you think of additional questions. Also, try asking the respondent if he can suggest further questions you should be asking and if he has any questions he wants to ask you.

Recording Interviews

To get the maximum benefit from interviews, the researcher should write down the information he has gathered. He might take notes during the interview, especially for interviews using structured questionnaires. Sometimes, however, the researcher feels he must not take notes during an interview because it would inhibit frank responses. In this case he should make notes as soon after the interview as possible. Researchers tell numerous stories of the race to any immediately accessible private place to spend several hours frantically writing up or tape-recording every aspect of an interview before it fades from memory.

If rapport with a respondent is good and if the topic is not confidential, the researcher may elect to tape-record an entire interview. Small battery cassette recorders are mobile and unobtrusive. But taping interviews has several shortcomings. Foremost is the time-consuming problem of transcribing the material so that results can be analyzed. A transcription takes at least twice as long as the original interview; even the best typists cannot type as fast as people speak. Another problem with taping is candor. If the interview probes for sensitive information, respondents presumably are even less willing to divulge such evidence in the presence of a tape recorder, which could implicate them. Thus before taping an interview, the researcher should decide if he really needs a verbatim report. For decisionmaking and many other topics, it may not be necessary and may hinder frankness. Transcripts may be worth the effort if the respondents' attitudes are central to the research. Verbatim records enable more subtle nuances to be captured.

If he intends to use a tape recorder, the researcher should inform the respondent of his intention, but no advance permission to use it is necessary. He might simply walk in for the interview with the recorder in view and after introductory remarks state matter of factly that taping is easier than taking notes and that no one else will hear the tape.

Observing

Observation has been developed into a precise skill, as revealed in Selltiz and others, *Research Methods in Social Relations,* pp. 205–17, on which we have relied heavily in developing this section. As with interviewing, the better informed the researcher is before undertaking the field work, the more productive his efforts are likely to be. Thus in observing social situations, he should find out all he can about what he is likely to see. He should also plan (1) what to observe, (2) how to record his observations, and (3) how to check their accuracy. In observing groups, the researcher might consider:

1. the participants and their relations
   a. what role does each of them play (critic, supporter, mediator, and so on)?
   b. what kinds of informal interaction take place among them (who sits where, who talks to whom)?
2. the seating and its impact
3. official and unofficial purposes of the group, and its norms or values (its rules of the game)
4. the activity
   a. what issues are raised or not raised (what issues do not come up that you might have expected to be raised)?
   b. how are the issues handled (do they lead to conflict or consensus)?
   c. what are the patterns of influence? what factions exist?
5. frequency and length of the activities

Often the researcher prepares tally sheets in advance for recording certain standard observations, such as attendance, voting, and seating patterns. In some cases he may take additional notes while observing without interfering with the action. In other cases, he may have to defer note-taking until immediately after observations.

To check on the accuracy of observations, the researcher might:

1. compare notes with a transcript of the session (we have remarked previously about the time-consuming aspect of transcripts)
2. arrange for two or more people to observe the same group and compare reactions
3. consciously develop his ability to separate descriptive material from interpretive material
4. ask respondents to look at his record of the session and compare their impressions with his.

Once he has completed his planning and is actually observing a social situation, the researcher has many options to heighten his awareness of what is going on. He might pick up any written material available (seating charts, brochures, and so on); he might ask people in his vicinity how they interpret what is happening, and afterward he might talk to the participants.

PARTICIPANT OBSERVING

Styles of participant observation are even more difficult to describe than styles of interviewing and observing. The role you establish within the group is the central consideration of this method. How much do you want to get involved? Will you give advice and state your opinions? Or will you try to stay detached, a neutral participant? The role you decide on will influence your analysis and the reactions other people have to your analysis. If you become a partisan, then those who disagree with you may disregard your results. On the other hand, if you try to stay detached, all parties may become suspicious. In any circumstance the subjects will attempt to test you, to see whether you are really interested, whose side you are on, what your motivations are.

A journal is essential for participant observation. Record in it both your observations and your interpretations, preferably on a daily basis. Write down not only what you see happening and who tells you what but also your thoughts about these events. You can easily become deceived into thinking that you will remember such details without a journal. But unfortunately important points fade from memory or are changed to fit with later perceptions. Thus a journal is important for all field work projects and particularly for participant observation. The journal provides the basic raw material for future analysis.

No matter what field work methods you use, an important general rule is to compile your findings frequently. This means going over your records to see what trends and gaps are revealed in the accumulating data. Frequent compilations enable researchers to reassess their plans and to sharpen the focus of their future work. Reassessments also prevent the buildup of an immense backlog of data which becomes so intimidating that the researcher continuously postpones the crucial task of analyzing data.

We now turn to such analysis, along with how its results may be used.

analyzing and using the results

5

This chapter considers the analysis phase of field work. What does the researcher do with what he gets? We have already indicated that analysis of results goes on simultaneously with field work; the researcher should frequently review the records of his interviews, questionnaires, and observations while they are in process, watching for patterns and relationships as he compiles and synthesizes the evidence. He should keep a running record of his thoughts during these initial analyses—ideas to pursue, possible explanations, points to be checked, and tentative outlines of the final report.

ADVICE

So far we have described projects as if a researcher has to rely completely on himself. Yet during all stages of field work advice from others can be helpful. Professional researchers typically talk over projects with their colleagues, soliciting suggestions on problem formulation, data collection, and analysis. Students, too, should be able to get help from both peers and instructors. We oppose the "pay and split" approach to field work, which sends students into the field as soon as they enroll in a course and never offers any guidance, taking on faith that learning will occur. We believe that educational institutions have an obligation to offer periodic opportunities for students to discuss their progress and get help for field work projects. Such support can be given informally, on a one-to-one basis during office hours; or it can be given formally in lectures or small group discussions of field work. There are many logical stages for such assistance: as the project topic is being formulated, when research designs are being prepared, after field work is under way, and when results are being analyzed. Advice should help students maximize the benefits of their field experiences by providing new perspectives on the process.

ENDING FIELD WORK

Advice and initial analyses do not eliminate the necessity of deciding when to stop collecting data and start completing the project. Just as field work may have been difficult to start, it also may be hard to stop because more items can always be investigated. But time must be put aside for concluding a project since it often takes as long to analyze and write up results as to gather them. It is usually better to stop too early (knowing that further information can be gathered later in the field) than to collect more data than time permits using. If the concluding stages of a project are extremely rushed, the results probably will not do justice to any of the material.

We recommend stopping field work as soon as periodic compilations show that findings are beginning to take shape. At this point the researcher should stop collecting new data, devoting himself to analyzing assembled data. Only after the analysis is nearing completion should he resume field work and even then such work should be focused on filling in specific gaps harmful to the analysis.

CONTENT OF FINAL PRODUCT

In developing a research design and executing the field work, the researcher should have in mind the shape of the final project. He should gradually begin to see pieces of the answer to his problems and how these pieces fit together. In other words, an outline should begin to emerge.

The outcome of field work could take many forms, such as a written report, an oral presentation, a dramatization, role playing, or a film. The value of creative final products can be enormous. This chapter discusses only the written report, but hopefully some people will want to go beyond that.

Results of field research typically are presented as follows:

1. statement of the problem
2. description of research design
3. consideration of field work methods
4. analysis of results
5. interpretation of results and conclusion (Selltiz and others, *Research Methods in Social Relations*, p. 9).

Analysis and interpretation of results are discussed here because they typically cause the most difficulty.

Analysis versus Description

After accumulating a large amount of information, the researcher is tempted to describe everything he has learned and to let the reader draw his own conclusions. Such reports are diaries or journalistic presentations, but they are not analytical. What then constitutes analysis as opposed to description?

Analysis seeks to discover the components of a phenomenon, the basic elements that underlie and explain a complex, changing issue. A researcher looks at his evidence to see what the essential factors are. For example, after gathering interview data on how a particular piece of legislation was formulated and passed, he seeks to identify the key parts of the process, which would explain why the legislation took the shape it did. In other words he looks at his evidence to draw conclusions about his central question. If his question is how the Civil Rights Act of 1964 got passed, he analyzes the data to find the main factors accounting for that act. Thus he does not have to describe all the details of the legislative process or all the idiosyncratic stories he heard about the Civil Rights Act. His report presents evidence relating to his central question, and the report explicitly discusses the conclusions he has reached by weighing the evidence.

Analysis may involve more than identifying component parts. It can entail, for example, finding relations between parts, comparing parts, seeing patterns, and discovering inconsistencies and gaps. Such elaborate operations serve to underscore the contrast between analysis and description. Analysis sifts the evidence to find basic elements; description merely conveys the details of the evidence.

ANALYZING DATA

The techniques for analyzing data range from very simple to extremely complex. Research methods and project design largely determine the appropriate techniques. Because we are not emphasizing survey methods, we shall not discuss sophisticated statistical techniques for analyzing data. Instead we shall indicate some of the less complicated ways of sifting evidence.

Establishing categories to be used to organize data is essential to analysis. Appropriate categories depend on the research questions and underlying hypotheses. If, for example, the central question is how public health personnel carry out their jobs, the researcher might ask staff members what their jobs involve. Then he would try to categorize their responses. If some respondents stressed fulfilling the duties prescribed by their organization and others talked primarily about serving clients, he might use two categories—client-centered and organization-centered public health workers. Selecting appropriate categories for responses from unstructured interviews is particularly difficult, although not impossible.

After selecting categories, the researcher must assign evidence to the categories. Which responses are client centered; which are organization centered? This process is called coding. Then he must tabulate the number of cases in each category.

The essential task—finding relationships between categories—still remains. Cross-tabulations show cases occurring in two or more categories. For instance, the researcher might want to discover the characteristics of client-centered public health workers. How many also fit into another category, such as registered Republicans? How many are under thirty years of age? Such cross-tabulations may suggest important patterns. For example, if a large proportion of the client-centered public health workers is under thirty, the researcher might want to explore the data further for possible explanations of the pattern. Did they all go to the same school of public health? Did they all come from certain types of families? Or does the amount of time they have been in the organization account for the pattern?

Cross-tabulation is one way of analyzing the data. The researcher might also want to determine the typical case within any category or set of categories; the distribution of variations; the differences between variations; and the explanations of variations. Once he starts looking closely at the evidence, he might be surprised how many different ways he can use the information. The tabulations and manipulations he chooses to make will depend on what he wants to know.

INTERPRETING DATA

Analysis of evidence is not enough. It must be accompanied by an interpretation of what the findings mean. What is their significance? What lessons do they suggest? What conclusions can be drawn from the analysis?

The researcher shows the implications of his results for existing knowledge on the subject. He indicates which generalizations his findings support and which they challenge. He thus links his analysis with pre-existing bodies of knowledge. In other words he integrates empirical evidence with conceptual frameworks. For example, if his question is how university decisions are made to give students financial aid, his analysis should reveal the major factors influencing those decisions. Yet if the report stopped there, its real potential would not be realized. A full interpretation would consider what these factors reveal about larger issues, what they illustrate, or into what larger category the case fits. For example, the influential factors might be indicative of how the university operates as an organization, or the case of financial aid might be one part of a larger question of how distributive organizations work.

Some people enthusiastic about field work dislike this interpretive phase because library work is again important, just as it was in formulating the topic, hypotheses, and field work methods. They may think that field work will get them out of the library, but this notion is only partly true. Field work does involve gaining new data, but to be valuable the data must be compared with the existing literature on the subject. A sophisticated field work project is a synthesis of field experience and intellectualization. It uses concepts that can be read about in libraries to bring understanding and order into real life situations. The data give new impetus and shape to the inquiry, and the inquiry gives greater significance to the data.

Another feature of interpreting results is indicating what aspects of the topic need further study. Research heightens the researcher's awareness of how many things he does not know. Experienced researchers do not try to conceal their ignorance; they capitalize on it by pointing out gaps in the evidence and suggesting ways of eliminating them by further work. They know that familiarity with a topic may qualify them to assess what questions are important to ask in the future. Finding an important new question is often the most difficult step in the search for knowledge.

Using Results Not Neutral

Even though social scientists have an obligation to be as neutral as possible in analyzing and interpreting the evidence, they must not delude themselves into thinking that their results can be neutral. If the results do have impact, they will not be neutral. They will be used by people for their own ends; they may well be used as evidence in disputes. Many social scientists have experienced the anguish of seeing their results employed to make cases with which they disagreed. For instance, a social scientist committed to a negative income tax finds some shortcomings in pilot programs to test this approach. When the results are published, they are frequently cited as evidence against negative income tax plans.

Awareness that results are not neutral does not solve the problem. We do not adhere to the belief that a person should manipulate his findings to prevent others from manipulating them. Yet during the process of analyzing and interpreting results, the researcher should keep in mind how others are likely to use his report, and he should indicate clearly in the report what he feels the proper uses are.

Writing the Paper

Data analysis and interpretation provide the answers to the research question. After he discovers his findings, the researcher must concentrate on communicating them effectively: He should state at the beginning of his report the specific research question, the main argument, and how he intends to support it. First he should get clear in his mind what he wants to communicate, what his main point is. This message is his theme, or thesis, which unifies the analytical and interpretive sections of his report. Just as he chose a focused question while designing his project, he should formulate a focused answer. The report must give a concise answer to the central question that shaped his research. One way he might test whether his thesis is clear is to state his main point in one sentence. Often students ramble on and on when asked to tell what they learned from their field work. This rambling shows that they have accumulated bits of information but have failed to integrate them into a central thesis.

Once he is clear about the content of his thesis, the researcher must then develop a logical argument to support that position: He should decide what subtopics he will need to cover and how they should be organized to explain his thesis. All the parts of his report should logically relate to one another and help to support or explain his theme. In other words he should build a case to sustain his argument. The components must add up to the main thesis. It is not enough to offer a smattering of interesting analytical and interpretive comments. A haphazard assortment of information does not suffice. An outline may help to develop a logical plan of relating the parts of an argument.

The thesis and supporting argument do not have to be earth shattering. The theme may be tentative or weak, such as all the data suggest it is too early to tell whether this reform is working, or the results of this study are mixed and no conclusive answer emerges. But the conclusion must be clearly expressed and firmly supported.

Other ways of communicating effectively are drawn directly from the rules of English composition. The necessity of adhering to these rules in a social science paper may come as a surprise. Invariably students who find their papers marked with comments about composition ask, What is this, an English class or something? Or they say that because they knew what they wanted to say, they should not be criticized if they failed to communicate effectively. They may respond to comments about lack of clarity by saying, What I meant was such and such. Then they rephrase their ideas in excellent fashion. The point is that the clear formulation should have been used in the original paper. Just having an idea straight in one's head is not sufficient; the writer must also convey it to the reader. If the reader does not understand a point, the writer—not the reader— must make changes to convey his ideas.

There are many guides to effective English composition. See, for example :

JACQUES BARZUN and HENRY GRAFF, *The Modern Researcher*
SIR ERNEST GOWERS, *The Complete Plain Words*
WILLIAM STRUNK, JR. and E. B. WHITE, *The Elements of Style*

One of the most important suggestions is to rewrite material several times. With each draft the author seeks to improve his manuscript. He cuts out needless words such as "in order to" and "it is thought that" to achieve conciseness. He strengthens the logic of his argument by making the relations between his main ideas clear.

The ideal procedure is to put a finished draft aside for a while before revising it. This procedure enables the writer to look at the material more objectively when he returns to it. Unfortunately, because writers often lack confidence in their abilities, their fear of getting a poor evaluation prevents them from making the best use of their skills. They wait until the last moment and then write something in a frenzy simply to be done with the dreaded task. Daniel Moynihan has aptly described "the work of a harassed undergraduate hoping against reason that his senior thesis, compiled in three horrendous nights of scissors, paste, and black coffee, will be accepted on grounds that he will otherwise not graduate" (statement in United Nation's Committee III on the Report on the World Social Situation, October 7, 1971).

Using Empirical Evidence

So far our discussion about writing applies to both library and field work papers. The effective use of empirical evidence, however, merits special attention.

Data from field work must be integrated into the argument to show what evidence supports a given statement. The most typical failure is the use of evidence merely as illustrative anecdotes. For example, a student interviewed five social workers to get their opinions on welfare reform. Then, instead of fully analyzing their responses, he wrote a paper summarizing the arguments for welfare reform (since it was a short paper the arguments were general, sounding like newsmagazine summaries) and occasionally using quotes from the interviews. His paper would have been much stronger if he had concentrated on social workers' attitudes toward welfare reform, analyzing the interviews to find clues to why social workers felt as they did, what differences their responses indicated, and what their attitudes suggest about the prospects of reform.

It is not easy for people lacking experience in field research to use empirical evidence fully. They may have been so intimidated by the printed word that they think only publications can be cited to support their arguments. For instance, a student who had had several revealing interviews about a piece of legislation with state legislative sponsors and leaders of opposing interest groups asked, "What kind of evidence can I cite? Do I have to find an article that makes the points?" The response was, "Of course not, your evidence is in the interviews."

The mechanics of linking evidence to arguments vary. The first part of the paper explains the field work, and sometimes an appendix is placed at the end of the paper, where all field sources of information are listed and evaluated. (This appendix, like an annotated bibliography, can prove useful to others who want guidance on studying the topic and to the author if he later decides to pursue his research.) Then the analysis and interpretation of evidence incorporate supporting data into the text. For example, if the argument is that certain groups were beneficial, such a generalization should be followed by an indication that twenty-five of thirty respondents said they thought the groups were beneficial. If this form of citation makes the argument too fragmented, footnotes and tables can be used to give the empirical details.

The use of evidence to support statements does not entail revealing the identities of respondents. Both introductory descriptions of field work and later citations can be written to protect the anonymity of sources, whenever necessary. For example, the researcher might say that he interviewed six top-level officers from specific companies, or he might withhold the names and locations of the companies and give only a general description.

The necessity of linking evidence with arguments does not preclude speculation, which goes beyond the evidence. Inevitably the researcher will want to make statements he cannot support with his evidence. This is defensible as long as he acknowledges the gaps in his evidence.

Determining Proper Form

Many conventions exist about the proper form for scholarly manuscripts. When correctly used, such rules increase clarity and consistency, but sometimes following the rules becomes an end in itself. A useful general guide to proper forms for all parts of papers is Kate Turabian, *Student's Guide for Writing College Papers.* A more detailed guide by the same author is *A Manual for Writers of Term Papers, Theses, and Dissertations.* For a complete description of bibliographical and footnote references, see Peyton Hurt, *Bibliography and Footnotes.*

The preparation of tables also requires attention. A table should be titled, and each column of data should have a heading and should indicate the unit of measurement. Other suggestions for tables are found in Mildred Parten, *Surveys, Polls, and Samples,* pp. 477–84. Oliver Benson, *Political Science Laboratory,* chapters 2 and 3, contains further advice about tables, as well as helpful information on graphs and charts.

Actual Writing

Understanding all the points described in this chapter will not substitute for actually sitting down to write. Most writers know well the many subterfuges they use to put off that task—sharpening pencils, searching for some indispensable object, and running to books to check unnecessary details. Jacques Barzun and Henry Graff explain in *The Modern Researcher,*

Writing is for all of us an act of self-exposure. Writing requires that we create some order in our thoughts and project it outside where everybody can see it. The instinct of self-protection, of shyness, combines with the sense of our mental confusion or uncertainty to make us postpone the trial of strength (p. 382).

Barzun and Graff provide various useful suggestions for overcoming the initial inertia and creating momentum for writing. They suggest setting aside regular periods of time and using a quiet place for writing. Begin writing as soon as some part of the topic starts to be formulated in your mind. Remember, modifications can be made in later drafts, so do not be afraid to write less than perfect prose in the first attempt. Keep writing once you have started, and do not stop to check words or facts that can be filled in later.

Some people are so tense about writing that they see papers as punishment that they must endure, and they fail to take advantage of the educational opportunities. One way to overcome the tension is to concentrate on communicating what you have learned, on weaving together the ideas in the most effective manner. This emphasis changes the focus from How will other people evaluate my work? to What can I do to convey my ideas as well as I can? The latter emphasis makes criticism from instructors and other readers useful because it helps the writer to judge whether he has conveyed what he had hoped to communicate.

Maximizing Project's Impact

Field work projects can be valuable not only to the researcher but also to other people. Such projects can be used for more than self-education; they can educate others. Students sometimes fail to take their work seriously enough. Because they are expending energy, they should try to maximize the impact of their efforts.

Respondents usually appreciate receiving copies of the research report. They are interested in seeing what conclusions the analyst reached, because often they do not have time to think about issues objectively. Students sometimes are apprehensive about showing papers to their respondents, especially if conclusions are negative and if further contact with the participants is desired. In such cases they might show only a summary highlighting suggestions for change. Whenever possible, they should show respondents a preliminary draft of the paper, soliciting their comments about changes for the final version. Respondents often provide revealing new information once they see the data researchers have obtained. They may be anxious to fill in gaps or tell new details to strengthen positions they favor.

Showing results to respondents is not merely to satisfy their curiosity. It can also influence their behavior. Studies may uncover information the respondents were unaware of, or they may show issues in new ways which lead the subjects to change their behavior. The changes may not be dramatic, but they are nevertheless interesting possibilities. Respondents use many student papers as part of their strategy to change the operations of an organization. A member of an organization can point to the student's conclusions to support his own arguments within the agency.

Researchers may also show field work results to other interested parties, such as journalists, public officials, employees, and teachers. Ralph Nader relies heavily on student research. Professors often use insights gained from student papers when they are serving as consultants for agencies. Researchers may also use their field work results as the basis for filing complaints with appropriate public bodies, such as the United States Equal Employment Opportunities Commission. But they are obliged to use their results only in ways consistent with the story they told respondents to get their cooperation. For example, if a researcher says he is conducting a study for his school course work and the respondent says, "All right, but this is not for the newspapers," then the researcher must not violate that trust.

Students may also want to develop their work for future publication to reach a wider audience. Because social scientists conceive of social systems in so many different ways, quality student work can make significant contributions to fill the gaps in understanding. Students have written a number of books and articles. John F. Kennedy's *Why England Slept* is a well-known example. And even if a field work study is not published, it may be useful to other students and researchers in their work. For assistance in preparing manuscript copy for publication, see Marjorie E. Skillin, Robert M. Gay, and others, *Words Into Type*, and University of Chicago Press, *A Manual of Style*. Also for interesting insights about the glories and miseries of refining a manuscript and seeing it through the editorial and publication stages, see Jacques Barzun, *On Writing, Editing, and Publishing*.

Regardless of what uses are made of projects, students should discuss their work with other students. This exchange increases the value of a project by communicating its findings to others and also enables students to learn from one another, to benefit from the work done by others. The format for this exchange may vary. Students may simply be encouraged to read papers of other class members. Having copies available for class members facilitates this process, but papers also may be available for reading at a specific location. Students may be asked to present their findings to the entire class, or they may hold small group discussions on papers about similar topics. Interchange of information among students often increases motivation. They see what serious work some people have done, what interesting experiences are available, and how their efforts compare with those of other individuals.

Field work combining participation and analysis is a valuable way of learning about the real world. This form of participation can be worthwhile not only for individual learning but also for society. The social value can occur for several reasons: the direct impact the researcher has on the attitudes or behavior of the subjects of his study, the influence his findings have on his subjects, the contribution of his findings to a body of knowledge about the topic, and the impact of the field work experience on the researcher's subsequent attitudes and behavior. Clearly the social impact is problematic and depends greatly on the researcher's motivation, effort, and skill. Field work is more than a mere academic exercise: it offers students the opportunity to develop intellectual, emotional, and personal traits that will enable them to contribute to the development of society.

In the next chapter, excerpts from student field work projects illustrate well the diversity, creativity, and imagination possible.

sample field work projects

6

Samples of field work papers can serve as useful models and supplement the generalizations made in the preceding four chapters. In classes we encourage students to read and discuss each other's papers so they can learn about a range of topics and see ways of improving their work. Student reactions to this approach have been highly enthusiastic, although after such discussion sessions they invariably express sympathy for the instructor who has to evaluate such diverse projects. In this chapter we present condensations of four student papers to show the variety of possible topics, empirical evidence, and modes of presentation.[1] (Some ways in which such papers may be used to effect change were discussed in Chapter 5.)

In some cases we have modified the papers to fit the purposes and format of this book, but we have also tried carefully to retain the tone of the papers by using the students' exact words wherever possible. We have paraphrased, shortened, or deleted various sections and also made anonymous many references to specific organizations, place names, and people. The most drastic change has been the elimination of all footnotes. Although we would have liked to show how the authors support their arguments with citations of empirical evidence from their field work or related literature, such citations would be unwieldy in

[1] We wish to express appreciation to the following students whose papers we have used: Jeff Brudney, Arthur Christa, Christina Narr, and Ron Tasoff.

this book, as would be the annotated bibliography that accompanied each paper.

The length of the original papers varied from five to twenty-five double-spaced typewritten pages, depending on the authors' time and interest, and the instructors' requirements. All the papers ask a specific question and answer the question in a thesis supported by empirical evidence, but the quality of analysis and presentation varies.

The first two papers focus on actual organizations—a state agency and a federal agency—and raise different questions about them—questions of secrecy and mission. Following the excerpt of each paper, we briefly assess the writer's treatment of the issue.

The first paper considers secrecy in the decisionmaking process of a state public utilities commission.

*student paper—secrecy and a state public
utilities commission*

Problem Statement

The purpose of the following discussion is to examine the extent to which secrecy surrounds the decisionmaking process of a state public utilities commission, concentrating especially on the effects of changes that have occurred in this process during the last two years. Naturally, since the commission does not operate in a vacuum but daily affects the lives of millions of citizens in a highly tangible manner, it is important to consider the implications that a high degree of secrecy may have.

Field Work

My field work has been extensive, time consuming, and rewarding. Since I encountered a paucity of material dealing directly with the subject of secrecy in the public utilities commission, I relied heavily for much of my information on personal contacts with those who possess thorough knowledge of commission operations. I utilized primarily three forms of contact. First, I wrote many letters requesting information. Second, I made numerous telephone calls, a detailed recitation of which could only bore the reader. Third, I was fortunate to be able to conduct interviews, ranging from one-half hour to two hours, with five individuals who are especially knowledgeable concerning the commission: a consultant to the state legislative committee on public utilities, a former member of the commission, an administrative assistant to the commission, a high-ranking member of the commission's financial staff, and its information officer. I conducted the last three interviews in the course of a single day spent at the commission headquarters. I also attended a hearing called to determine a utility rate.

Findings

Prior to 1970 the public utilities commission employed basically a two-stage process to determine utility rates. The initial stage began when a representative of a utility filed an application for a rate increase with the commission. The commission then scheduled hearings to consider the increase where anyone could attend and/or testify, and notified the public of their location and time through newspaper announcements. Although both a commissioner and a hearing examiner were assigned to each case, usually the latter presided over the hearings, which were similar to law court proceedings. . . .

After the public hearings, the examiner and commissioner assigned to a particular case developed a proposed decision, which they submitted to the agency's division heads for comments and approval. This action signaled the commencement of stage two in the decisionmaking process. If the division heads had no objections to the proposed decision, they signed the report; if they did not agree with its provisions, they indicated their disagreement to the commission by withholding their signatures. Each week the commissioners met in conference with the division heads, their high-ranking staff, the executive secretary of the commission, and a number of other high-level agency officials to assess commission opinion on pending cases and, when necessary, to examine the reasons underlying the refusal of any division head to sign a report. After discussion with this group of 25 to 30 officials . . . the commissioners voted on each proposed decision in full view of the officials present at the weekly conference. . . .

In 1969 the commission began to consider instituting changes in its decisionmaking process. . . .

Looking back at the changes in commission decisionmaking policy that have occurred over the last two years, I do not think that there can be any question that the public utilities commission has moved toward making its operations more secret. Although the first stage of its decision procedure, the public hearings, remains entirely open, the final stage has always been closed off from public view and has been increasingly removed from staff scrutiny as well. The commissioners have made a process that has always been highly secret, even more secret by deciding first to modify the system by which the division leaders indicate their disagreement with proposed decisions in such a way as to exclude the commission staff from a thorough knowledge of opinion throughout the public utilities commission; second to conduct its final vote on rate cases in the presence only of the executive secretary; third to eliminate him from their final deliberation; and fourth to diminish significantly the amount of time devoted to discussion between high-level commission staff and themselves. We now can and should examine the implications of secrecy in the commission's decisionmaking.

Implications

The secrecy of the commission's operations leads to a host of consequences frequently noted in the literature of public administration. Perhaps the most evident of these consequences is the fact that since the commission reaches its final decisions in complete privacy, the actual influences on the decisions are not known and many interested groups may not be consulted. Reducing staff involvement in the commissioners' deliberations blinds the commission to available alternatives and information. Submerging the final stage of its decisionmaking in darkness from the public denies the contribution an informed public can make to executive policy. Furthermore, it prevents public appraisal of the government performance, which is an essential attribute of democracy. These consequences are a high price to pay for enabling the commissioners to eliminate "wasted hours" and to speak more freely without the inhibition created by the presence of the staff or public.

If efficiency and candor were the only rationale underlying commission secrecy, the state legislature probably would not have guaranteed this agency complete freedom to open and close meetings as it chooses by exempting it from legislation requiring the business of public agencies to be conducted in public except for personnel matters. Commission spokesmen, however, offer two further justifications, which may explain the actions of the legislature. First, commissioners feel that discussion of decisions in public prior to a ruling could harm the economy. . . . Second, they maintain that the commission is a quasi-judicial body, and as such it is fully entitled to the privilege of executive session.

One consequence of the secrecy that surrounds the public utilities commission activities became immediately apparent to me in the course of my research: the lack of information readily available to the public describing the actual operation of the commission. To complete the task of piecing together the decisionmaking process and reconstructing the changes that have taken place in it during the last two years required the accumulation and synthesis of a great body of information— much of it contradictory and confusing—gained through five interviews, innumerable telephone conversations, and many letters. Such effort can hardly be expected of the public; as a result, it is largely uninformed, an undesirable condition in a democracy. . . .

Since public utility commission officials cannot legitimately argue that the nonpolitical nature of this agency justifies the secrecy, how can they justify it? On the basis of their belief that secrecy is essential to prevent economic dislocation? Or that it is necessary to increase efficiency? Or to ensure candor? . . .

These gains in effectiveness are important, but as Francis Rourke points out in *Bureaucracy, Politics, and Public Policy,* effectiveness is not the only criterion by which we must judge the performance of the public utilities commission or any other bureaucratic agency—we must consider its responsiveness as well. The price secrecy exacts in the public utilities commission in the interests of effectiveness is very costly. Secrecy reduces the amount of alternatives and information available to the policymakers; it masks administrative blunders and the assignment of responsibility; it makes it more difficult to reverse errors in administrative policy; it impedes public appraisal of executive performance. Perhaps most serious of all, secrecy prevents intelligent public scrutiny. The reader must decide whether the effectiveness secrecy presumably promotes for the public utilities commission is worth the price.

assessment of paper on
public utilities commission

This paper is strong because it poses a significant, interesting question and presents a concise, unified answer based on empirical evidence. Look how this aim was accomplished.

The question is focused. The author does not ask a general question, such as, How does the state utilities commission function? He poses a specific question about function: How much secrecy is involved in decisionmaking, and what implications do changes in secrecy have? A precise question forces analysis rather than mere description because the author has to examine much data carefully to find pieces contributing to an answer.

The paper is well presented. The thesis that increases in secrecy have been harmful is clear and is supported by a unified argument. The field work is described well, and the data on secrecy in decisionmaking are analyzed, although much of the analysis is not included in our excerpt. The author discusses increases in secrecy, explanations of why they occurred, and reactions to them.

Note that the author does not burden the paper with extraneous information on the formal structure and history of the agency. That information is not essential to the question, even though the author probably learned a great deal about its structure and background while doing his research. In discussing implications, the author relates his findings to the larger issue of secrecy in all administrative agencies. He shows that secrecy in the public utilities commission is not a unique case but part of a larger topic—the tendency of decisionmaking in large organizations to be insulated from pressures so that effectiveness may be increased.

The quality of the empirical evidence is also good. The author contacted both proponents and opponents of increased secrecy, people inside and outside the organization, staff and board members as well as a legislative person. Observation of a commission hearing supplemented the interviews. These diverse sources of information overcome the tendency to discover only one point of view. If time had permitted, additional interviews with clients and legislators would have strengthened the paper.

It is always easy to see shortcomings in other people's work. This paper has no empirical evidence about the effect increasing secrecy has had on the actual decisions made. Although the author presents evidence of people's reactions to the changes and speculates on the impact of these reactions on the agency's effectiveness and responsiveness, he has not measured the actual impact. He could have indicated the need for such evidence even though he did not obtain it himself. But at least he does not pretend to have such evidence. In discussing implications, he speculates about impact rather than demonstrates it. As long as one is aware of the limitations of the evidence, such speculation can be valuable, suggesting interesting empirical questions for further study.

The next paper looks at a federal organization and uses interviews with regional office personnel and people who deal with that office.

student paper—an analysis of the U.S.
environmental protection agency's mission

This report examines the mission of the U.S. Environmental Protection Agency. By mission I mean not only certain goals set by law, but also how people associated with this organization interpret these goals and the manner in which they attempt to achieve them. To understand better these factors and others concerning power and internal organization and how they relate to mission, it is helpful to close the books and go into the field.

First it is useful to examine how the agency was established since some of its organizational problems originated at that time. And as will be discussed later, organization is closely related to EPA's mission.

Formation

On July 9, 1970, an executive order established the Environmental Protection Agency, which was to be formed by amalgamating fifteen components taken from the Atomic Energy Commission and the Departments of Interior; Health, Education and Welfare; and Agriculture. The object was to create a single interrelated system dealing with pollution.

The Director of an EPA regional office said that "good riddance" was the feeling most of the parent agencies had about losing sections to EPA. But there are reports that some agencies were reluctant to part with managers, scientists, and laboratories. By February 1970, EPA still was not certain which components belonged to the agency, and some feared the parts did not add up to a whole agency.

Some officials view EPA as a proving ground for two approaches to bureaucratic reform: functional grouping of an agency's activities and decentralization. Originally there were supposed to be five topical offices (water, air, radiation, pesticides, and solid waste), but instead functionally organized divisions were set up (enforcement, planning, management, and research). Power was decentralized to ten regional offices, which initiate court action against polluters, deal with state pollution officials, and award grants to states and municipalities. . . .

Power

EPA's legal authority originates from three sources: the Environmental Policy Act of 1969, which empowers the agency to issue environmental impact statements concerning government programs and legislation; the Refuse Act of 1899, which allows the regulation of discharge of industrial wastes into navigable waters through a permit system; and the Clean Air Act of 1970, which allows EPA to enforce federal water and air quality standards if the state is derelict in this duty.

I interviewed people in the regional EPA office to find their opinions on the agency's actual power. They indicated that the agency's name is too encompassing, since the agency does not have any control over land use or population control. Instead they saw the agency as a pollution control authority, which had been given only limited legislative authorization. The result is that the agency has few control mechanisms and cannot do as much as it would like, but the "name says too much and thus the public thinks we can do anything."

People who work in organizations that deal with EPA had widely varying views of EPA's mission and power. A steel company official told me that EPA was certainly powerful because it can shut industries down. He didn't know if the agency has caused a profound change but said that the public opinion and legislation behind it have. He said industry is aware that it is going to have to work on environmental problems and that this will have certain costs. An oil company executive said that so far EPA had not had an impact on his company but that the company would have to spend money to fight pollution, not because it was worried about fines but because it didn't want to lose business. . . .

assessment of paper on environmental
protection agency

The question raised in this paper about a national agency's mission and the idea of investigating the question by looking at people's perceptions of the mission and the actual operation are both good. We have included this paper because it shows that the national government can be a subject of field study when one does not have access to its offices in Washington, D.C. The interviews with clients of the agency (only a few of which are included in the excerpt) include public and private conservation groups as well as private industries and other public agencies, such as the U.S. Park Service. The diverse perspectives show the complexities of interorganizational relations.

This paper is not as strong as the preceding one, however. The author does not specify what he means by mission or how the various subtopics such as power relate to mission. In the first paragraph he implies that power and internal organization have implications for the agency's performance of its mission, but he does not make those connections explicit. Thus he does not tie together the various subtopics to support a precise answer to the question he poses at the beginning of the paper. He fails to show what the agency's organization and power prove about its mission. The author probably could formulate a strong thesis that would unify the paper, but he did not actually do so.

Rewriting could improve the presentation of his material. In revising, the author should also add a description of the field work he did (the appendix in the original paper did give a list of interviews but did not specify length or content). The author's generalizations about the national agency go beyond the evidence he presents based on interviews at only one regional office. He needs to formulate generalizations more firmly supported by his data.

The next paper concerns a segment of the population rather than an organization.

student paper—a problem of ideology: a retired section of a city

I'd like to begin this paper by saying that I had a difficult time trying to get the people in the retired section of this city to participate in the interviewing. They were suspicious of me and uneasy in my presence. It led me to believe that old people are really impossible to "reach" if you're young. To be honest, they acted like they hated my guts. But, in truth, I think that it's just that they could almost care less about the politics in this country. They're old and angry at or scared of America's active rioting, inquisitive, demanding youth and minorities. Those who did consent to be interviewed, of which there were nine, still desired that the personal facts about their individual lives not be made "public" in a paper written by a university student. It probably would have been boring anyway. That simply means that I have no information about their economic, historical, and occupational backgrounds. What conclusions did I draw about their political ideology?

I decided that these retired people are tired. They've had active lives, and they now wish to just sit back, be relieved of all pressing problems, and enjoy the remainder of their lives.

Their ideologies demonstrate this. Either they are blocking out the racial crisis in their city or they do not know about the situation, which I don't really believe to be the case. The same applies to any political facet in America; to them, everything seems to be well in control. And if there is present a dispute, disturbance, or general imbalance in the city, in the nation, it certainly isn't the fault of America's democratic governmental procedures. You see, it's just that according to one woman, "People are never satisfied with what they have." I asked her "Well, what do you think the reason is that they are not happy?" Her reply was typical of my group: "I suppose that people are just greedy by nature."

My group of people expressed a certain pride in having "the right to vote." They feel it to be some "award" the government is handing them. I wanted to know how they would use their vote to benefit themselves or the group they are part of. The general answers ranged from "to keep people who get out of line in this country from causing violent trouble" to "by keeping the general peace here." One man said that he had voted Republican in every election since he was able to cast his first ballot, and he isn't about to vote on any other party ticket no matter how worthy the candidate seems. That really depresses me. I mean, people in this country really do abuse the vote like that—over and over again.

I asked them how they would define power. They didn't like the question but answered it by saying it was "the ability to control things." I wanted also to know if they thought that some groups possess more power than do other groups. They agreed with that but thought it didn't matter because it was only fair that "the majority rules" and "people who have themselves in a bad position, haven't tried to help themselves climb out of it," and therefore, "deserve to be right where they are."

With that I went on to political parties. They again pointed out what a great society this is because "there is a choice between two able men in an election." . . .

I was also interested in finding out what they thought about the treatment of Black Panthers by city policemen. "These lawbreakers must be kept under control by any possible forceful means if necessary." "They were causing trouble and deserved the punishment they received." But punishment that severe? "Of course, anyone breaking the law has to be subdued; he is aware of the consequences as are we." So I guess you might say this age group is for law and order—no matter who suffers by it as long as it isn't them. . . .

So far I would say that a dominant ideology is appearing. They are conservative and not too worried, or not worried at all, about their futures. They're safe. They're not too worried about minorities or minority needs or demands. One said, "They must be patient. It takes time to . . ." I guess you can see that these people didn't do a thing for me. In fact, they really fixed a strong opinion of themselves for me to think about. It is evident to me that these ideas—political ideologies—stemming from this age group are directly aiding America's negligence of such race situations, students disturbances, and so forth, which we have all over the nation today. . . .

assessment of paper on
retired people's ideology

This paper is included because it studies a segment of the population by asking a focused question about retired people's beliefs. In addition, the paper presents an explicit thesis that the retired respondents have conservative beliefs and are content with the world. The author also makes good use of quotes from his interviews and indicates an awareness of the attitudes respondents had to the interviewer. (It is easy to forget the mutual interaction between interviewer and interviewee;

each person is forming impressions of the other and adjusting his behavior accordingly.) However, the paper does not follow a logical outline and therefore has a rambling quality, circling around the theme of conservatism. And the bias of the author is so pronounced that we might wonder whether he could perceive accurately what the respondents' beliefs were, or if his mind was closed to evidence he might not wish to consider. This doubt is heightened because in his analysis of the interviews, he does not indicate any divergence of views among his subjects. Could nine people have identical views on all the issues covered in the interview? Or did the researcher fail to notice existing differences? If the homogeneity was as great as he indicates, the author should have speculated on why it existed since we would not ordinarily expect responses from nine people to be so identical.

The final paper deals with a process rather than an organization or a segment of the population.

student paper—planning a school for autistic children

This case study focuses on a series of planning meetings that took place in a small midwestern city. A group of parents of autistic children met with local mental health professionals to design a school to meet the special needs of their children. Similar discussions must take place somewhere in the country nearly every day. But a close look at these talks indicates that they raised one of the enduring questions in political analysis—What is authority, and who ought to have it?—and an interesting problem of public policy—How well can a single organization carry out conflicting responsibilities? The question of authority remained unresolved in this case, as it does in the literature, but it merits consideration merely because it lurked in the background of such mundane discussions. The policy question remained unresolved also, but it is more amenable to immediate solution; therefore, a proposal is offered.

Data for this case study are derived from my participation in the planning process. As a staff member of a private organization, I was brought in as a consultant and was, therefore, involved in most of the major discussions.

Situation

A small group of parents of autistic children formulated plans for a school which would include a full-day program, enough teachers hired for a minimum of two years to allow one-to-one treatment, a psychiatrist and a psychologist both half time; and a full-time social worker to coordinate home, school, and community programs. The parents wanted the school to be run by a parent-controlled board of directors, which would be responsible for all significant decisions in both policy and administrative matters.

The parents met with various professionals for a series of planning discussions. The mental health professionals included staff of the local office of the state program for community-centered mental health services, university faculty members, and staff of the school operated by the county association for the mentally retarded. The professionals' response to the parents' plans was simple and unambiguous: "That's impossible." This reaction was buttressed by several arguments. The professionals said there was no need for a psychiatrist on the staff. It was unrealistic, they argued, to expect to find a permanent staff in a transient university community. Their ultimate argument was financial: the parents' program just would not be funded because it called for too much money for too few students. But the professionals urged the parents to modify their plans so that the school for their children would operate in cooperation with the existing school managed by the county association for the mentally retarded, sharing quarters, administration, training, and funding. Such cooperation would be looked on with favor by funding agencies, perhaps resulting in more funds for both schools.

The parents balked: they wanted little or no association with the school for the retarded, for they were deeply afraid of the stigma they felt the school carried; they continued to insist that only a child psychiatrist could minister to their children's needs; and they insisted on retaining control of staffing. As the deadline for funding proposals grew near, these issues remained unresolved, so no proposal was submitted.

Authority

Several months' effort by hard-working and good-willed adults, then, resulted in a stalemate and, as far as the children were concerned, no progress whatsoever. This section will be devoted to an investigation of why so little was accomplished.

A major factor, of course, was the parents' naïveté about the conflicting orientations among the mental health professionals. That there could be bitter conflict over the nature of autistic children's problems and raging battles over the techniques of the cure never entered their minds. The parents were also naïve on the question of funding. But disagreements over mental health procedures and funding were not of crucial importance, precisely because they were a result of the parents' naïveté. As the parents became more sophisticated, they became willing —and able—to compromise.

The really significant conflict involved areas in which the parents were rather sophisticated, aspects of the plan about which they were most informed. These aspects of their plans raised—in one way or another—questions of authority. The parents sought a weak administration, while the professionals insisted on a strong one. . . . The parents wanted to retain control over the staff. . . . And they resisted collaboration with the school for the retarded, sensing that they might be absorbed by the larger organization, losing more and more control as the process continued. . . .

There can be no question of evil intent—or even a lack of goodwill —on either side. The parents felt they should be accorded ultimate authority over their children's lives and planned their school with this conviction in mind. The professionals, however, considered many of the parents' demands incursions on their professional integrity. To become a professional is not merely to undergo extensive training, it is also to accept certain responsibilities and duties. Just as some behavior is proscribed, other activities are prescribed; and to allow any of these prescribed duties to be taken over by laymen is ultimately unprofessional.

Thus two different—although equally honorable—approaches to the problem of authority clashed here. The result was perhaps unfortunate, for the school would have served legitimate needs. But this was not a case where any school would have been better than none: if the parents had acceded to the professionals' arguments, they would have gained a school by sacrificing themselves. Their need for self-respect, a self-respect they equated with legitimate authority over school affairs, cannot be lightly dismissed.

Policy

The state program for community-centered mental health services is admirable in many respects. The local offices of this program make facilities and expertise available to communities throughout the state. But these local offices are also responsible for evaluating community mental health proposals and recommending to the state's funding agency which proposals should receive funds. An adverse decision on a proposal by the local office meant almost certain doom. The parents in this case were obliged to continue negotiations with the local office of the community-centered mental health services even though they sensed strong opposition, for the office spoke for the funding agency. The parents could not say, "Well, we disagree on this, we're going to submit the proposal our way and hope that the state will accept it." The local office represented the state, and there was no effective appeal from their ruling.

It is probably inevitable that parents clash with professionals over who exercises effective authority in a school of this type, for the differences in perspective are too deep to be glossed over. It is not necessary, however, that this battle be fought before the allocation of funds. The state system in this case leaves new programs at the mercy of local professionals, whereas a more equitable situation would entail the allocation of funds on the basis of merit as determined by an outside investigator. . . .

assessment of paper on planning a school

We have included a long excerpt from this paper (as we did in the public utilities paper) because it is well developed and reports insightful observations. It presents an analytical answer to a focused question about the implications of a planning process for authority and public policy. Instead of simply describing the conflict over school plans, the author analyzes the significance of that conflict for certain issues. In so doing, he shows what the case illustrates and thus links it with larger themes. His footnote references to relevant literature on authority, planning, and professionals are not shown.

The other aspect of this paper to which we want to call attention is the method of gathering observations. This student was a participant in an organization. Because he was a member in that organization he had access to special information. And for the purposes of his research he took on the added role of participant observer, analyzing a process in which he was participating. We can easily overlook the potential of such research. Many students who are interns, employees, or volunteers are participants in organizations or activities that could provide the basis for interesting studies such as this one if they could see the possibilities and were willing to analyze the experience.

Our assessments of these student papers are not meant to be definitive but suggestive of aspects worth considering. Although agreement on evaluating good papers is difficult, superficial, poorly presented papers are usually easy to spot, and consequently we have not included any such "horrors."

We have purposely avoided the issue of how formal the presentation should be. The paper on retired people is informal and conversational. Whether this style is appropriate depends on the audience—some settings call for impersonal reporting; others do not. But either way the paper may still be analytical and well presented.

All the papers could have been improved if there had been time for rewriting and collecting more evidence. More systematic research would be needed to provide firm support for the generalizations posed. But the authors have participated in observing interesting and real situations, and their attempts to make sense out of their observations were success-ful. In all likelihood they will remember the experience and what they learned from analyzing it long after they forget other aspects of their education.

introduction to role playing cases

In an era when more people want to participate, this book explores several kinds of participation. After the initial chapter considered some of these forms, chapters 2 through 6 concentrated on field work, which allows students to get *out of the classroom* and participate in the outside world. As researchers they take part in a real life situation and analyze their experience. But students can also participate *in the classroom* by means of role playing cases.

The second section of this book consists of five cases that involve participation in two ways. First, the cases ask students to play the roles of various parties in a conflict and to act out the situation. They debate the issues from their assigned points of view according to the scenario presented in each case. They then discuss what happened in the role playing and why it occurred, thus analyzing the process in which they have participated.

Second, the cases describe conflicts arising when people with different values and interests participate in society. The cases show many kinds of people participating in different ways in diverse issues. For example, the medical school case pertains to the issue of where such an institution should be located, but in addition various individuals participating in the conflict formerly would not have taken part and are participating in new ways.

The role playing technique contributes to many types of learning.

It sharpens skills of expression, observation, and analysis. It also provides exposure to the complexity of real problems. This experience can increase understanding of the interests and feelings involved, the various pressures shaping the conflict, the strengths and weaknesses of various strategies, and the nature of the outcome. Role playing may also lead to new assessments of the different positions. For instance, someone who normally defends management in controversies with labor may modify his position after representing labor in a case, or vice versa. Viewing a situation through different eyes may reveal reasons for certain phenomena that previously had seemed nonsensical and may suggest new problems and needs for reform. Role playing may also contribute to new perceptions of strategies for change and their impact.

Role playing can also teach the "fundamentals" of many subjects. A more traditional way to teach these essentials is to present the basic items in some logical sequence that proceeds from simple to complex. Most textbooks follow this pattern. A shortcoming of this traditional method is that the fundamentals have been abstracted from real situations; if students do not readily see the connections between the fundamentals and problems of interest, they may not be motivated to learn. We prefer to present the real problems—to plunge the readers into issues —which can give students a reason for learning the fundamentals they need to know to deal with these problems. For instance, the poverty board case depends on some familiarity with the council–manager form of government. The case incorporates enough information about that form so that students may understand the case. Thus in role playing the case the students learn about city managers. The bibliographical suggestions at the end of this book allow students to delve more deeply into case materials.

Role playing resembles gaming and simulation exercises, but it is simpler and more flexible. In brief, gaming and simulation have more elaborate instructional material and place heavier responsibility on the person in charge of the activity. They are concerned with quantifying inputs and outputs and predicting outcomes. At times the use of computers is necessary for calculations.

We have selected participation cases that illustrate important domestic social conflicts: the kinds of physical and social facilities that should be provided for ghetto areas, the control of professional organizations such as police departments and schools, the relative importance of major components of transportation systems, and the basic characteristics of regional governments for metropolitan areas. The cases involve attempts to influence the action of policy bodies and administrative agencies such as city councils, boards of education, state legislatures, and federal departments. They raise issues of interest not only to political scientists, sociologists, and economists but also to a wide range of professionals in the fields of social work, public health, and planning. The cases are based on actual events and have been selected to illustrate a variety of important issues existing in different settings. They have been kept anonymous, however, so that no one using them can gain an unfair advantage over other members of the group by doing extra background reading on the actual case.

The same format is used for each case. First, a description of the situation reviews the details of the case—the problem, the action taking place, and the reasons for and the reactions to it. Then an outline of the underlying issues in the controversy indicates how the action may be analyzed and what factors need to be weighed in reaching decisions about the problem. Next a brief discussion of the background of the case explains the legal and historical implications of the problem.

Directions follow for role playing the case. In each instance a list of roles and procedures is given. The procedures section describes what the arena of interaction is—a hearing or television debate, for instance— and what the specific question is for the role players. The procedures section subsequently gives the agenda for the interaction among roles. Each case specifies that the instructor assigns roles (several people can play one role, depending on the size of the class) and sets time limits for various steps in the procedure. The instructor may, of course, modify the roles and procedures in many different ways to fit the interests of the class. Prior understanding of modifications by all players is the only requirement. Once the class has agreed on the roles and procedures, the role players need to meet in small groups to work out their plans.

The subsequent section of the role playing directions elaborates on the content of each role player's part, describing what he does during the enactment of the agenda and what point of view he has. The players need to be familiar with the instructions for their own role so that they can behave spontaneously during the actual role playing rather than merely read from the instructions. Elaboration of the parts is a valuable aspect of role playing as long as it does not change the basic facts of the cases. Role players usually benefit from reading instructions for other roles so they know what views the others in the case will have. (The opportunity to read others' positions in advance may seem to be an unrealistic aspect of the role playing situation, but it is parallel to a real experience: participants often know the views held by other participants.)

The final section of each case indicates questions for discussion. They are suggestive rather than exhaustive, designed to encourage thought rather than to test for "right" answers.

The cases can be used in numerous ways, even though they are displayed in a role playing format. In addition to being used for student participation in role playing to increase empathy for the real participants in real life situations, they may serve as "readings." In the latter way, they may be employed for classroom discussion of conflict resolution, as a basis for analytical student papers, and as a springboard for lectures that will give attention to specific ideas in the cases.

a state as negotiator in a medical school controversy

7

the national government, a city, a medical school, and the black community

SITUATION

In 1967 one of the nation's largest metropolitan areas had the full array of familiar urban problems, particularly inadequacies in health care, education, employment, and housing. In its central city the number of blacks had tripled since 1950, and although they now made up almost two-thirds of the population there, they did not constitute a majority of the voters in the core municipality, and only one Negro, representing the central ward, was on the nine-member city council. The mayor had been elected in 1962 with strong support from black voters after many terms as a Democratic congressman. He was reelected four years later when a Negro was his opponent; by that time black support of the mayor had declined.

In 1962 the mayor started to urge that a medical school take over the municipal hospital. After four years had elapsed, the board of trustees of a college of medicine and dentistry, a public educational institution located in another large urban center in the same state, informed the United States Public Health Service of the Department of Health, Education and Welfare (HEW) of its plan to request funds to build a new medical school and hospital. The central city tried to interest this medical college in relocating in an urban renewal project in its central ward. The construction of a medical complex was seen as a way of easing the city's health and unemployment problems and rehabilitating a deteriorating area within it. But in June 1966 the college's site selection committee chose a suburban location, ostensibly because of the availability of more space (132 acres in contrast to about 50 acres in the central ward).

The city decided to entice the college with an offer of a 185-acre site without actually intending to give this much land; the city felt the college was using the limited amount of acreage in the city's original offer as a subterfuge for its reluctance to locate in the ghetto and would not finally ask for so much space. The thirteen-member Democratic state legislative delegation, the governor's office, and many private organizations pressured the college to locate in the city. In June 1967 the college agreed to locate there if the city would provide 57.5 acres in the central ward by March of the next year and 100 additional acres on eighteen months' notice. The state quickly passed the necessary enabling legislation, and the city council voted to accept the contract.

In July 1967 extensive rioting took place in the inner portion of the city. The outrage among blacks over the college's decision to locate a medical school and hospital in the ghetto contributed to these eruptions. Earlier two community groups—the Area Planning Association (APA) and the Committee Against Negro and Puerto Rican Removal (the Committee)—were formed to protest this decision. The APA sought to find legal means to reduce the site size; the Committee was headed by a teacher who stressed the importance of pressuring HEW and Housing and Urban Development (HUD) officials. But these groups were not broadly based and did not have much impact until after the riots.

Following the riots, several other parties became highly active in the medical school controversy. A state agency on local affairs, which had been established to help local governments deal more effectively with urban problems, acted to reestablish communication between the city and the blacks. The national Department of Housing and Urban Development had to decide whether to approve the Model Cities application by the city. The city demonstration agency had developed the application, which called for the medical school to furnish improved medical services for the community. But the medical college's application to HEW for construction funds had a different tone since it made no mention of training, employment, or outpatient services. Furthermore, the Model Cities application did not provide for adequate citizen participation in the development and implementation of its proposed program.

At the request of APA, the National Association for the Advancement of Colored People (NAACP) in December 1967 lodged a formal complaint, which asked that HUD reject the college plan because the plan did not meet the requirements of the Model Cities legislation. The director of the state local affairs agency also urged that HEW and HUD give the matter serious attention.

As a result of these actions, HUD decided to withhold approval of the Model Cities application until consulting HEW. The latter found that no urban medical school used as large a site as the college had requested and that no correlation existed between acreage or size of a student body and quality of a medical school. When HEW carried out its traditional site visit, the visitation team for the first time anywhere included observers from HUD and the local community. During the field inspection and discussion, major state and medical college officials made favorable statements about the application for school construction funds. The ghetto representatives, however, asked for a smaller site than 157.5 acres, the use of neighborhood people in construction jobs, and the relocation of displaced persons.

Following the visit, the undersecretaries of HEW and HUD met to work out the details of a joint letter to the governor of the state, which had been discussed with all the concerned parties. The letter set forth criteria that had to be satisfied before the two federal departments would approve the college's plans:

1. Proper acreage must be determined in accordance with the provisions of the Model Cities legislation designed to improve the conditions in the ghetto and must consider the social impact of removing land from residential use.
2. The medical school must provide increased health services to the ghetto.
3. The medical school and the city demonstration agency must insure citizen participation in the development and implementation of plans.
4. The city must provide for relocation of displaced persons.
5. Residents must get jobs in the construction of the medical school.
6. Residents must be trained for positions as paraprofessionals in health fields.
7. Planning for additional facilities must be linked to the Model Cities program.

In addition to Model Cities and Public Health Service regulations, the college's plans also had to comply with HUD urban renewal procedures. The city's housing and renewal authority had to redesignate a small parcel of land (11.5 acres) in the previously approved urban renewal project from residential to public use before the land could be conveyed to the college. The rest of the land (46 acres) had to be subjected to the usual urban renewal requirements of public hearings and city council and HUD approval. In January 1968, HUD in a letter to the director of the city's housing and renewal authority said it would approve conveyance of the 11.5 acres only after a public hearing and agreement on the undersecretaries' criteria.

The availability of federal funds thus depended on the parties' working out ways of meeting the undersecretaries' criteria. But the college and the ghetto representatives made no progress: the college did not accept the ghetto negotiators' claims to be spokesmen for the black community or their demands for the college to use only seventeen acres, put ghetto representatives on its board of trustees, and give the ghetto a voice in faculty and curriculum matters. To overcome the suspicions of the college and the black community of each other, the involved state officials called for a series of public meetings to determine the views of the larger community. The public meetings were to alternate with informal technical meetings where the parties would develop positions to be presented at the public meetings. The state felt quick action was necessary, because the college might decide to abandon this proposed site in the face of increasing student and faculty transfers to medical schools in other states, and the national government might give the funds to other states where agreements had already been reached.

ISSUES

1. Who should make decisions about the site location of a state-supported medical school? Government officials (national, state, local—elected or appointed), medical professionals, the people of the entire city, or the black community where the school will be located?
2. Whose interests and values should have priority?
3. How should the conflicts be resolved? How should interests be balanced?
4. Should the goal of a medical school be to train doctors or to help solve the social ills of the ghetto?
5. What makes a person qualified to speak for the entire community? What makes a person qualified to speak for the black community?

BACKGROUND

In recent years the number of federal grants for social programs available to states and local agencies has greatly expanded. These grants have increased the frequency and complexity of interactions between federal, state, and local organizations. The medical school controversy is a good illustration of the web of intergovernmental and interorganizational relations involved in federal grants.

Three types of grants are present in the case: Model Cities, urban renewal, and hospital construction. The goal of Model Cities grants is to improve the quality of life for ghetto dwellers by physical and social renewal programs for designated areas. Money is made available to cities for planning and implementing comprehensive programs that are responsive to local needs and overcome the fragmentation of existing programs in these areas. The Model Cities legislation in 1966 called for cities to create city demonstration agencies. These agencies are responsible for developing proposals that conform with HUD Model Cities guidelines, obtaining city approval of the proposals, submitting them to regional and central HUD offices, and then implementing approved proposals under federal supervision with federal money and local matching funds.

Urban renewal grants antedate Model Cities grants and have emphasized physical rather than social renewal. The objectives of the 1949 Housing Act were to eliminate substandard housing and to redevelop communities. In local areas urban renewal programs are run by local public authorities, separate from city demonstration agencies. Urban renewal and Model Cities programs are also administered by separate offices within HUD. With federal approval, local public authorities can buy and clear large amounts of land, selling the land to private developers who agree to build according to urban renewal specifications. HUD guidelines require public hearings and city government support at various stages in this process.

HEW also administers a wide variety of federal grants, including the hospital construction grants cited in the medical school case. Proponents of a specific urban project typically look for funds from a variety of public and private sources. Thus attempts to obtain grants for the medical school from both HEW and HUD are not unusual. But the diverse requirements attached to the different grants greatly complicate efforts to deal with urban problems.

Directions for Role Playing

Roles

1. Negotiating team of nine blacks (elected at a community meeting)
   three from APA
   three from the Committee
   one minister
   two from New Legal Services Project (war on poverty project funded by the Office of Economic Opportunity)
2. President of the college

3. City representatives
   Director of housing and renewal agency
   Director of city demonstration agency, also representing the mayor
4. State representative
   Chancellor of state board of higher education serving as mediator
5. Federal representatives
   one from HUD
   one from HEW
6. Audience
   For example, representatives of central city business groups, labor unions, black community organizations, and residents of the affected area

Procedures

The various role players take part in two different types of negotiating sessions, first a public meeting and then an informal meeting. The goal of the negotiations is to reach agreement on a medical school plan that fits the federal criteria. To achieve such an agreement, the negotiators must reach decisions on the following subjects:

1. How many acres will the college get?
2. What kinds of citizen participation will the city demonstration agency and the college allow?
3. What guarantees of minority employment in the construction of the hospital will they give?
4. What guarantees will there be for relocation of displaced persons?
5. What kinds of health services and training for ghetto residents will the college provide?

Actual negotiations usually occur over a long period. The sequence of negotiations is drastically shortened here.

1. Public Meeting
   a. State representative opens meeting and explains procedures
   b. College, city, and blacks give opening statements
   c. Involved parties ask questions
   d. Statements and questions are presented from the floor
   e. State representative makes closing statements
2. Informal Meeting
   a. State representative asks parties to agree on a procedure for the informal meeting
   b. Parties attempt to agree on a compromise medical school plan including acreage, participation, and employment
   c. State representative summarizes areas of agreement, which will be announced at a later public meeting

The instructor assigns roles (number of people assigned to a specific role varies with class size) and establishes time limits appropriate to the class schedule. Each group of role players should meet briefly before the negotiators start, to plan its strategy.

Instructions for Roles

Each participant may elaborate on the facts presented to fill in gaps but may not change the facts as presented in the situation.

1. State representative
   a. Open and moderate the public and informal meetings
   b. Announce procedure for the public meeting: After opening statements by the main parties (limited to x minutes each), questions will be accepted from all the parties, including state and federal representatives; then statements and questions will be taken from the floor (limited to x minutes each).
   c. Make sure procedures are followed so that all points of view are heard.
   d. Close the public session: the parties will consider the points heard and announce areas of agreement at the next public meeting.
   e. At informal session ask participants to agree on procedures: will the questions be discussed in order or will the parties first consider the areas where agreement is more likely, leaving the more difficult problems to be handled last?
   f. Ask questions and express the state's position (the college is needed in the city and will strengthen the state's system of higher education) in both informal and public sessions; suggest compromises and offer specific state assistance in the informal session.
2. Blacks
   a. Prior to public meeting decide who will speak and what priorities to attach to reducing acreage, obtaining health, employment, and relocation guarantees, and getting community participation. Decide on your strategy for both sessions: how much to demand and when, how much to compromise and when. Consider the effect of various strategies on potential allies; shape your strategy in view of the risk you run if the medical school does not come to the city or if no agreement is reached and federal funds are thus not forthcoming. Also decide how to handle disagreements within the black negotiating team and those between blacks in the audience and the team.
   b. At public meeting present an opening statement explaining your position.
   c. Questions you might ask the college: Why does the proposed school want more land than most of the best medical schools in the country? How can it train good doctors without exposing them to the needs of the ghetto? How can the college know the needs of the ghetto without letting the ghetto residents have a voice in the affairs of the school?
   d. Questions you might ask the city: Why did the city housing and renewal authority originally agree to redesignate the 11.5 acres without

a public hearing? Why were all the original agreements with the college made without consulting the ghetto community? Does the mayor hope to weaken the black political power now that it no longer supports him? Is the college going to help the city's whites more than its blacks? Is the talk about participation merely an attempt to make minorities think they have a voice when really the final voice is in city government? Why does each government department say it cannot do anything about the problems and then pass the buck to the next? Why are you unreasonable, when you ask us to be reasonable?

3. College
   a. In the opening statement stress your desire to provide top quality medical education and your determination not to come to the city unless this is possible. Point out that the plan would require 57.5 acres now and perhaps more later for expansion (stress that you never wanted almost 160 acres now; that was long-range plan).
   b. In the opening statement or the question period get across the following points of view:
      (1) When the city was trying to get us to locate here, it appeared that all the business, ethnic, and government groups wanted us to come. We thought they were representative; now other groups are claiming to be the proper spokesmen.
      (2) Originally the city did not require us to provide community health and other services. Now it has changed the ground rules.
      (3) Public officials and minorities have used the medical school issue to raise other issues, such as housing and unemployment, which are not central to medical education.
      (4) We resent being dictated to about land and programs by people in HUD, HEW, the city housing authority, the city demonstration agency, and the community, who know nothing about medical schools. Experts have told us that the plan we presented to the national government is one of the best they have seen.

4. City
   a. In the opening statement explain that you had to make an attractive offer to the college to entice it away from the suburb. Since the college will help blacks, compromises were necessary.
   b. Stress the following points:
      The redesignation of 11.5 acres was so minor as not to require a public hearing. Our housing authority knows about land use, and if the college had accepted our advice things would have worked much better. Federal regulations require the city to follow certain procedures to get money, and we therefore have to conform even when the requirements seem unreasonable. Conflicting stipulations and procedures in HEW and HUD result in time-consuming red tape.

5. HUD and HEW representatives
   a. Explain that the federal departments have worked closely together to set reasonable requirements; since their money is involved, they are naturally concerned that it be used wisely. Deny any conflict between HEW and HUD.
   b. In informal session help state representative find acceptable compromises. Indicate inability to approve any agreements until clearance has been obtained from "higher-ups."

6. Audence—sample of possible comments
   a. Black resident: All you "Uncle Toms" up there who say you represent me, I did not vote for you. You talk tough now but you will sell us out in private sessions.
   b. White resident: How come the "bigwigs" and the blacks get more time to talk than we do?
   c. Black resident: How am I to know who to believe? Everybody tells me something different. All I want to know is whether I am going to get a fair price for the house I own when it is destroyed to make room for the college. I have lived in that house all my life, and it represents the only savings I have.

QUESTIONS FOR DISCUSSION AFTER COMPLETION
OF ROLE PLAYING

1. What were the values and interests of the participants?
2. What strategies did they follow, in both the public and informal meetings? How effective were they?
3. What pressures were operating on each participant and how did these pressures shape their performance?
4. Why did the conflict occur? Could the issues have been handled without conflict?
5. Were the procedures followed throughout the controversy fair? Who benefited from them?
6. Was the outcome fair? Who won? Who had the most power?
7. What changes in procedures or outcome do you feel would have been desirable? Why?
8. What do you think might occur after an agreement is reached? How fast would funds be made available? How could the parties circumvent the agreement? Would the election of new city, state, and federal officials change the results?
9. Are public meetings efficient? What arguments might be used in their favor? What arguments might be used against them?
10. How did the class handle the role playing? How could the roles have been performed differently? What oversimplifications probably occurred in the role playing (for example, did each federal department seem to have one clear position so that conflicts between departments were minimized)?
11. What were the class's reactions to role playing? What are its advantages and disadvantages for education?
12. How did the class handle the *discussion* of role playing? Comment on both the content and the process of the discussion. Did the class listen to various points of view? How did it deal with differing opinions expressed in the discussion after the role playing? Did the class members help clarify what the comments of various participants meant? Did people help summarize and direct the discussion?

a city council debate

local poverty agency versus the city council

8

SITUATION

This case takes place in a large city of more than 250,000 people, about a third of whom are blacks and Mexican-Americans. For many years the city has had a reformed government: a council–manager system, with at-large nonpartisan election of the nine councilmen, one being the mayor. The municipal reform movement in the early part of the present century viewed this structure favorably; its belief was that this type of organization would replace corrupt bossism with expert concern for the general good.

This city has also been in the forefront of developments in the war on poverty. In December 1961 it received one of the first Ford Foundation "gray area" grants to improve conditions in the inner cities, which are portions of large urban centers characterized by poverty and physical disintegration. The city manager's office originated and administered the resulting city interagency project. In 1964 the mayor and the city manager directed the staff of the interagency project to develop a municipally-run poverty program so that this city would be in a position to be one of the first to receive funds from the national Office of Economic Opportunity (OEO). The proposals were submitted to Washington in October 1964 and funded shortly thereafter. The poverty agency created in this city was called the Economic Development Council (EDC). It consisted of a 29-member board appointed by the mayor, plus a staff in the city's department of human resources.

As the city's poverty program developed, many tensions arose between the city government and EDC. These tensions became most pronounced during the controversy in 1966 over an EDC proposal for a police affairs committee. To understand this conflict, let us discuss the development of EDC.

Because this city was early in starting a poverty program, the structure for administering the project was designed without the necessity of conforming to federal guidelines or clear community demands. But as such guidelines and demands were articulated, the structure gradually had to be modified.

The major modification concerned the power of community groups in relation to EDC. At the initial meeting of EDC in December 1964 the members of this council appointed by the mayor consisted of representatives from labor, management, minority groups, and civil rights and religious organizations, but the council had no representatives from the four target areas of greatest poverty. These four areas, which had been specified in the proposals of 1964, included more than 100,000 people, with over half of them designated as impoverished. The areas included two-thirds of the city's poverty population, over three-fourths of its black inhabitants, and three-fifths of its Spanish surnamed residents. These areas were not directly represented on EDC, which also did not provide for area councils in these poverty pockets.

While attempting to operate programs in the four neighborhoods, EDC staff members called community meetings and discovered strong opposition to city-controlled antipoverty programs. People felt EDC had been organized without consulting target area groups. EDC members responded that leaders of six black and Mexican-American organizations had been consulted in the formation of EDC and that organizations and groups with low-income constituents were represented on the EDC board and could speak for the target areas. As a result of community pressure, however, EDC agreed in April 1965 to provide for resident participation by creating target area advisory committees (TAAC's) made up of democratically selected area residents and by having each TAAC send two representatives to EDC.

This move, however, did not quiet the criticism. TAAC's became increasingly dissatisfied with a role limited to advising. Questioning whether the poverty program was designed to serve the people or city hall, they demanded control over programs in their areas, veto power over programs not acceptable to them, and 51 percent of the membership of EDC and its executive committee. As antagonism grew between TAAC's and EDC, the EDC group became increasingly suspicious of the motives, capabilities, and representativeness of TAAC members. EDC's chairman pointed to a survey which showed that only one-third of the members of TAAC's came from families below the poverty line of $4,000.

At an evening meeting of EDC in February 1966, attended by more than 100 target area residents but with many council members absent, TAAC representatives united to get the council's approval of 51 percent representation for TAAC's (the vote was 11 to 7). At the next EDC meeting the chairman defended the existing structure and appeared to repudiate the agreement made at the previous session. Contradictory statements made by the regional OEO office heightened the confusion: first, the coordinator said that even though OEO does not require 51 percent representation for TAAC's the decision made at the February meeting should be implemented; several days later he said that the existing structure satisfactorily met OEO requirements.

The controversy led to the creation of a special committee to make recommendations on the proper relationship between EDC and TAAC's. In May 1966 the committee's proposals were accepted with surprising equanimity in view of the preceding controversy. The agreed reorganization provided for 20 of the 39 EDC members to be elected by the target areas, with the remaining 19 members to be appointed by the mayor to represent elected officials (3), business and industry (2), labor (2), private agencies (2), National Association for the Advancement of Colored People (2), Congress of Racial Equality (1), Negro business and professional people (1), Mexican Americans (1), American Indians (1), Orientals (1), and religious groups (3). It also called for 75 percent of the members of TAAC's to be low-income people and for TAAC's to be given increased powers over programs and personnel in their areas.

Several explanations have been suggested as to why the previously hostile parties were willing to reach this compromise. Opponents of TAAC's felt that the 75 percent poor requirement would prevent TAAC's from being dominated by militants, who might attempt to manipulate the poor to build up their own power, and that compromise was essential to prevent increased tension. Furthermore EDC members were willing to accept strengthening TAAC's because EDC knew that support of these committees would be needed in the developing confrontation with city hall over a police review board proposal.

The dispute over a police review board started in December 1965, when TAAC's were asked to take part in an examination of program proposals for 1966 (they did not exist when EDC screened the proposals of the previous year). When this proposal for a police review board (police affairs committee) was discussed, it was opposed by the police department, the city manager, and the district attorney, but supported by the EDC chairman (a black superior court judge). At the February 1966 meeting TAAC representatives united to get EDC approval of the police proposal despite city governmental opposition. EDC voted to submit the program to OEO for funding. Although OEO had already indicated the proposal was ineligible because it was not limited to serving the poor, EDC hoped to get money from the Ford Foundation, which had said it would only consider proposals for funding after OEO had officially said this organization was ineligible for OEO support.

The police affairs committee proposal called for the creation of a private corporation to operate a civilian review board to investigate citizens' complaints against the police in the absence of any official body fulfilling this function. The agency would have a 30-member board with three staff members. Hearings would be in private and include a police representative. The agency would not have official power but would simply try to help complainants get relief through existing channels. This proposal approved by EDC reflected widespread dissatisfaction with police performance in the inner city. Critics alleged numerous cases of misconduct and objected to the absence of minority policemen (only 20 minority people were in the police force of more than 600). The black leadership of EDC shared a strong interest in the proposal with TAAC's. The fate of the police affairs committee became a test of EDC's willingness to push for a project of deep concern to minorities and of the power of EDC in relation to city hall.

The police department consistently denied charges of misconduct and maintained its internal procedures were adequate for disciplining policemen; the police internal affairs section, make up of two white officers, considered complaints. And the city council had gone on record as opposing police review proposals in September 1965, both times by a vote of 8 to 1 with a black councilman being the sole dissenter in each case. This position was supported by the city's leading newspaper, which said a police review board would weaken police morale by permitting unqualified individuals to interfere in professional matters.

When the city council learned of EDC's approval of the police affairs committee proposal, it expressed anger that EDC, "a creature of our appointment," had supported the plan for a police review board without first checking with the city council. It asked the EDC director to appear before the city council and explain the action of EDC. At the March meeting the director said the police affairs committee was not a police review board; but the police chief disagreed, saying the committee was equivalent to a review board. The council was ready to reject the proposal but agreed not to act until EDC formally presented the proposal to the council with a request for expenditure authorization. The proposal, however, was never formally submitted to the council. The EDC staff was responsible to the city manager, who was in charge of presenting such proposals to the city council; he held the EDC proposal on his desk while the mayor attempted to avoid a direct clash between the council and EDC.

The mayor persuaded EDC to name a committee to work out a compromise such as a human relations commission or an ombudsman, if the city council would pass a resolution indicating the need for some action to improve police behavior. At the mayor's urging the council passed such a resolution in April 1966. But EDC went ahead and submitted the proposal to the Ford Foundation in May without city council approval, because the foundation had indicated it would consider the grant even in the absence of OEO action. Both the council and the mayor considered this action improper, and the council decided further action on its part was necessary.

ISSUES

1. Who should control the disbursement of money for poverty projects? Local or state government officials? Independent poverty agencies? Established private agencies? Indigenous groups? Would the answer be different if the funds were from national government rather than foundation sources?
2. Who should control local government agencies such as the police department? The professionals within the agency? Elected officials (councilmen or mayor)? City manager? People in the ghetto area? People in the entire city?
3. How should the conflicting views over who should have control be resolved?
4. Should the goal of the poverty agency be to provide supplemental services or to try to change established institutions? Should the agency cooperate with existing institutions or confront them?

BACKGROUND

Title II of the national Economic Opportunity Act of 1964 called for the establishment of community action programs that would mobilize public and private resources of an area to reduce poverty through "developing employment opportunities, improving human performance, motivation, and productivity or bettering the conditions under which people live, learn and work" (78 Stat. 508, Title II, 202a, 1 and 2).

These programs could be administered by either a public or a private nonprofit community action agency (CAA), but they must be "developed, conducted, and administered with the maximum feasible participation of residents of the areas and members of the groups served" (78 Stat. 508, Title II, 202, 3). Not until the end of 1966 did Congress specify that one-third of a CAA governing board must consist of democratically selected representatives of the poor. And only later was the creation of TAAC's encouraged, with the suggested membership of the poor set at 50 percent.

Community action agencies are responsible for administering the war on poverty in local areas throughout the country. These agencies plan and conduct poverty programs, subject to federal guidelines. For example, they screen project proposals from local groups that want federal funds for their programs. The CAA's decide which proposals to approve. These decisions are reviewed by the federal department responsible for the proposal (usually the Office of Economic Opportunity, Department of Labor, or Department of Health, Education and Welfare) and its regional office. In addition, approved proposals must be submitted to state poverty offices. If a governor objects to a proposal, the proposal will die unless the federal department decides to override the state's position. For simplicity in the present case, the role of the state in screening EDC proposals has been eliminated.

From the start of the war on poverty, conflicts developed over the purpose of community action programs and maximum feasible participation. Some people felt CAA's should approve programs that would provide services to help the poor adapt to the system. Others emphasized the need for programs to help the poor gain power so they could change the system.

Community action agencies do not have to rely solely on public funds. They often approach private philanthropic groups, such as the Ford Foundation, for support. When CAA's approve programs designed to increase the power of the poor, they may find that public bodies will not provide funds but that private philanthropies are more willing to experiment with such programs. Ford Foundation "gray area" grants in the early 1960s served as important models for the war on poverty. Once OEO funds became available to poverty areas, the Ford Foundation changed the criteria for its urban grants to avoid duplicating government efforts. The foundation looked for other approaches to the problems of the inner city. But when community action agencies are public agencies, as in the present case, support from private foundations does not eliminate the threat of opposition from public bodies. The government unit that creates and operates the community action agency may try to block certain types of programs even when funds for them come from private sources. This is the conflict we see with respect to EDC and the proposal for a police affairs committee.

At the time of this case the city, with a council–manager government including a nine-member council elected at large, had one black on the council, two Orientals, and the rest whites. The council hires the city manager, who is responsible for administrating city affairs. Many early advocates of the city manager form of government thought the city manager should be concerned exclusively with administration rather than with the formulation of policies. However, it is widely acknowledged today that city managers are deeply involved in both the formulation and the implementation of policy and therefore are political figures.

DIRECTIONS FOR ROLE PLAYING

Roles

1. Eight city councilmen
2. Mayor who is also a councilman
3. City attorney
4. Chief of police
5. Chairman of EDC
6. Regional representative of OEO
7. Audience
   For example, chairmen of TAAC's, members of the professional police association

Procedures

The role playing in this case takes place at a city council meeting where the councilmen are to decide what action to take on the community action agency's proposal for a police affairs committee. The following choices are open to the council:

1. Support EDC application
2. Support EDC application with modifications worked out by the compromise committee
3. Postpone action
4. Take no stand, but if Ford grants the money, do not interfere
5. Oppose the proposal and prevent any Ford money from going to EDC

The council meeting will be relatively open and informal. Not all councils work this way. Some councils make many of their decisions in private meetings held before the public meetings and strictly curtail discussion from the audience. The rationale is that issues should be settled on the basis of thorough study and rational discussion rather than as a result of heated public debate. The sequence of the council meeting follows.

1. Mayor's announcement of the EDC item on the agenda and explanation of procedures
2. Reports from the city manager and city attorney
3. Questions from the councilmen directed at the city manager and city attorney
4. Comments from the EDC chairman
5. Questions from the councilmen directed at the EDC chairman and the regional OEO representative
6. Comments from the audience
7. Discussion among the councilmen
8. Vote by the councilmen on the alternatives open to the council

The instructor assigns roles (number of people assigned to a given role varies with class size) and establishes time limits appropriate to the class schedule. Each group of role players should meet briefly before the council meeting starts, to decide on its approach to the issue.

Instructions for Roles

Each participant may elaborate on the facts presented to fill in gaps but may not change the facts as presented in the situation.

1. Mayor
   a. Announce that the next item on the agenda will be EDC's proposal for a police affairs committee. Then review the procedure for consideration of this item: First we shall hear a report from the city manager and city attorney; after that councilmen may question concerned officials, including the city manager and city attorney; next, the EDC chairman will give his remarks on the issue; then councilmen may question the EDC chairman and OEO's regional representative; next, councilmen will discuss the issue and vote on what should be done.
   b. State your (mayor's) position on the issue during the questioning of speakers and the council discussion: A compromise is necessary because a more effective poverty program would be possible if different elements in the city remain together. EDC needs city involvement and support, and the city can benefit immensely from the poverty funds.

Oppose the straight review proposal of EDC but also disagree with the police department's absolute refusal to make changes in present grievance procedures. Explain that middle ground would be ombudsman system, citizens' alert plan, human relations commission, inspector general either as a citizen or as a staff member of the police department, or even inclusion of civilians within the internal affairs division of the department.

c. Act as chairman of the whole meeting, calling on the various speakers and trying to prevent interruptions from the audience, explaining that they can speak only at the end of the consideration of the agenda item.

d. Call for motions at the end of the meeting, handle the voting on the motions, and announce results of the vote.

2. City manager
   a. When called on by the mayor, review the background as presented in the situation, which was presented at the beginning of this case.
   b. Present your recommendation that the council prevent any money from Ford going to EDC. Although this position may precipitate a crisis with EDC, do not permit inflammatory actions that will conflict with the policy of the city council.
   c. Then call on the city attorney to present his position.

3. City attorney. Present your opinion that the city council is trustee for all EDC funds and as long as the council's policy is opposition to a police review board, the funds cannot be used for that purpose. Remind the council that the city is the actual applicant and recipient of all funds—foundation and federal—given to EDC.

4. Councilmen
   a. Question all officials present—the mayor, police chief, city manager, city attorney, EDC chairman, regional representative of OEO.
   b. State your opinions, for example:
      (1) The poverty program is a headache; we do not want it. The funds it provides do not compensate for the problems.
      (2) The city council created EDC and it must follow us, but now it is threatening to become a second government. We must retain veto power.
      (3) How representative is EDC? It has a disproportionate number of representatives from TAAC's (one-third is the more usual proportion), and these representatives are not really responsible to anyone.
      (4) More study is necessary because the needs of the people in the ghetto are not being met. We set up a committee to work out a compromise, and we should not take action until the committee has had enough time.

5. Police chief. When questioned by councilmen, state your position that ever since the issue was raised the police department has been unalterably opposed to review boards. All the talk and the national publicity about supposed police brutality are giving the police department an undeserved bad image. The sooner the issue is disposed of by forceful denial, the better it will be for the police department.

6. EDC Chairman
   a. When called on by the mayor, state your position that you accepted the EDC chairmanship with the understanding that city hall would not

attempt to dominate the agency. EDC must have autonomy, including full policymaking power. If EDC does not have autonomy, it can no longer operate as part of the city. If the council takes the action recommended by the city manager, EDC will be forced to take drastic action of its own. But its purpose is not to conflict with city hall; if EDC has the necessary autonomy, it can supplement city hall.

   b. Defend the representativeness of EDC.

   c. Criticize the stalling tactics of the city manager, who is keeping the proposal on his desk, thus forcing EDC to go ahead and apply for Ford funds before action was taken on the original proposal.

   d. Defend the good faith of EDC on the compromise committee, and point out that the city council has never sent representatives to the committee as it was supposed to do.

   e. Give your opinion contradicting the city attorney's position on the legal aid society. The society finds that the city's relation to Ford is not the same as to OEO, and therefore the city cannot control funds to EDC from Ford.

7. Regional representative from OEO. When questioned by councilmen, equivocate.

8. Audience—sample of possible comments

   a. Chairmen of TAAC's. Attempt to speak; charge the council with trying to whitewash the issue; claim that EDC and TAAC's are more representative than the city council.

   b. Community people. Urge the council not to listen to the TAAC chairmen; TAAC's are not really for the people, just out for themselves.

QUESTIONS FOR DISCUSSION AFTER COMPLETION OF ROLE PLAYING

1. What arguments would the city council give to support its desire for control of poverty funds? What arguments would EDC give?

2. What could be some of the motivations behind the original proposal of the police affairs committee, which was presented to EDC?

3. What could be some of the motivations behind EDC's support of this proposal?

4. What are the possible explanations of the city manager's attitude to the proposal? The mayor's? OEO's?

5. What was the purpose of the councilman's questions—assistance in forming opinions or support for pre-existing opinions?

6. Who benefited from the procedures used throughout the controversy? What changes in procedures or outcomes do you feel are desirable? Why?

7. What factors influenced the council's vote on EDC's proposal?

8. Based on this case, does reform government seem conducive to the general good of the city? If not, what changes would be beneficial to the city?

9. Are public meetings efficient? What arguments might be used in their favor? What arguments might be used against them?

10. How did the class handle the role playing? How might the roles be performed differently? What might have been oversimplifications in the role playing (for example, were possible conflicts within EDC and OEO ignored)? How might the role playing vote differ from an actual city council's vote in such a case?

11. What were the class's reactions to role playing? What are its advantages and disadvantages for education?

12. How did the class handle the *discussion* of role playing? Comment on both the content and the process of the discussion. Did the class listen to various points of view? How did it deal with differing opinions? Did the class members help clarify what the comments of various participants meant? Did people help summarize and direct the discussion?

a board of education hearing on a teachers' strike

professionals versus decentralization

9

SITUATION

Until the 1960s many people felt that public employees would not strike because of prohibitive laws. But strikes by public employees have increased and caused growing concern. Recent years have seen strikes by municipal employees in San Francisco and Cincinnati, social workers in Sacramento, sanitation workers in Atlanta, policemen in Carbondale (Illinois), and teachers in many different cities.

One of the most complex public employee strikes occurred in a large metropolis in 1968 when a teachers' strike in violation of an anti-strike law closed the city's schools for over two months. The conflict did not involve salary levels or curriculum content but the clash of teachers' rights with minority demands for decentralization.

Minority students, blacks and Puerto Ricans, make up more than 50 percent of the school enrollment in this school district, even though minorities only constitute 27 percent of the city's population and less than 20 percent of the voters. Minority students at twelve years of age are on average two years behind other students. Minority teachers make up less than 10 percent of the teaching staff.

The school system of this metropolis is highly centralized, although the district is geographically vast and socially complex. The nine-member board of education is the formal policymaking body for the district. The mayor appoints the unsalaried members for staggered seven-year terms. A nominating committee presents a list of names to the mayor from which he makes his selections. Various interest groups in the city actively back favorite candidates during the nominating process, and board members are responsive to the organizations that supported them. In general the board has a reputation for being progressive and supportive of civil rights causes.

The board is not actually the initiator of policy, however. Like most lay boards, it is weak in relation to the professional staff, and it acts primarily as negotiator between the competing interests in the school system. These include internal groups such as the teachers' union (the recognized bargaining agent for all the teachers in the system), associations of principals and supervisors, and the personnel selection board. Important external groups include parents' associations, religious organizations, and labor.

In the 1960s certain groups called for decentralization of the school system to make it more responsive to the community. Several areas within the school district carried out a decentralization project involving the creation of local school boards. One of these areas, which will be called Woodacres, started its experiment in the spring of 1967 by setting up a planning organization, which included representatives of parents and the teachers' union. This group was recognized by the board of education and received a foundation grant to set up an experimental subdistrict. The group planned for a local governing board and the operation of local schools during the school year 1967–68 and selected an administrator for the subdistrict. The 24-member governing board was to include a parent and a teacher from each of the eight area schools, five community representatives chosen by the eight parent members of the board, two school supervisors from the district, and one university representative.

When the newly created governing board met in August 1967, it approved the administrator's recommendations for five principals to fill the vacancies in the subdistrict. The five people selected were not on the approved civil service list from which the board of education usually is legally required to make its personnel selections. But the local governing board chose these principals to fill a new category called demonstration elementary school principal, which had been approved by state education officials and the board of education. The local governing board also asserted its right to select teachers for the subdistrict. In response the teachers' union sued to remove the newly appointed principals on the grounds that they were illegally appointed, and it forbade its members to sit on local governing boards.

Meanwhile difficulties within the subdistrict mounted during the school year. Many assistant principals asked to be transferred from the Woodacres schools. The board of education met their requests, appointing personnel from the civil service list to replace them. The local governing board's requests for increased control over the budget were denied. Friction reached a peak when the local governing board took action against certain personnel, partly in response to complaints from parents and principals that many teachers and assistant principals were hostile to the decentralization experiment and were trying to undermine it. In May 1968 the local governing board voted, on the recommendation of its personnel committee, to remove six administrators and twelve teachers from the subdistrict because they were not sympathetic to the needs of the blacks in the Woodacres schools.

With union backing, the dismissed teachers and administrators insisted on their right to continue working in the Woodacres schools. The union demanded a hearing for the accused personnel where the evidence against them would be presented. Community people tried to prevent the dismissed individuals from entering the schools, insisting that the local governing board had the right to decide personnel matters without giving reasons. Union teachers in Woodacres did not go into the schools, saying that because the dismissed teachers could not go in, all the teachers were being locked out. The community viewed this action as a strike.

The mayor urged the superintendent of the school district to persuade those dismissed to accept reassignment to avoid continued confrontation. Some agreed, but ten teachers, all Jewish, refused and relied on the union to support them.

Various unsuccessful attempts to settle the dispute were made. The board of education met with representatives of the local governing board to try to get the parties to agree to arbitration. An independent negotiator presented a proposal for a settlement, which was rejected by the governing board. During the summer various members of the board of education met privately with the administrator of Woodacres and with the union president. However, no agreement had been reached by the time schools were due to open in September.

The decision of a hearing body, appointed by the board of education in May to consider charges against the dismissed personnel, had made a compromise settlement more difficult. In August the hearing body ruled that the administrator could not transfer any of the teachers involved. So the union and the board of education no longer felt they could yield on this issue. Since the local governing board voted to oppose the court decision, the conflict was now between the Woodacres board on one side and the union and the board of education on the other.

Just before the schools were to open, the union voted to strike because an understanding had not been reached on the teachers' rights in all decentralized subdistricts, including Woodacres. In the meantime the local governing board vowed to operate its schools with teachers hired to replace striking union teachers.

On the first day of school more than 90 percent of the teachers in the district were on strike, but Woodacres schools were open because the subdistrict had hired nonunion staff. Within a few days, however, the board of education and the union had agreed on a contract that provided for a binding district grievance procedure which would require subdistricts to present charges to a central panel of arbitrators. In addition the board of education agreed to order the ten teachers returned to Woodacres and to give back pay to the Woodacres teachers who had struck in support of their ten associates. Union members voted to settle the strike but authorized the executive committee to call another strike if Woodacres refused to abide by the contract.

On the following day the teachers returning to Woodacres were harassed. They were barred from entering the schools, their lives were threatened, and they were not given teaching assignments. Thus the board of education had to decide what action to take. If Woodacres were allowed to circumvent the contract that the board of education and the union had agreed on there would be a strike. A strike would mean that many students would be out of class and the pressure on the board of education to reach a settlement would be intense. But the Woodacres subdistrict would not experience this pressure because its schools would still be operating with the nonunion teachers.

ISSUES

1. To whom should the board of education be responsible—city government, parents, students, teachers, or the community?
2. Who should control education—an independent board of laymen, professional educators, elected officials, students? Who is qualified to decide education policy?
3. Should the governing of school districts be decentralized? If so, what powers should be given to subdistricts and who should control them?
4. Can decentralization of school systems threaten the professional autonomy of teachers? Will subdistricts violate due process and academic freedom?
5. Should public employees have the right to strike, or should antistrike laws be maintained and strengthened?

BACKGROUND

Before 1947 conventional wisdom suggested that public employees would not strike against the government. But after a Buffalo teachers' strike in that year, antistrike legislation was passed in approximately one-third of the states, including the state involved in the present case. The prohibition was based on the idea of sovereignty: government is the supreme source of authority with greater claims to the loyalty of its employees than other organizations, and therefore strikes are an attack on sovereignty and the public good. When antistrike laws failed to prevent strikes, penalties against violating unions were increased to as much as $10,000 a day.

Many school boards are totally independent of city government; they are in control of separate government units not linked to the city council or mayor for funds or personnel. In this case, however, the board of education is part of city government. The mayor appoints the board's members, and the city council must approve its budget. Like most school districts, this one also has links with the state education department, which sets certain standards and provides about one-third of the district's funds.

In this case the board of education selects the superintendent. Typically the choice of superintendent is the most important decision a school board makes. He is the chief contact between the board and the rest of the school system. He is the board's primary source of information and has authority for the day-to-day operations of the school district. The superintendent therefore is often the key figure of a school system. However, when public controversies arise, the school board may attempt to take a more active part and watch the superintendent more closely. Although the board may remove the superintendent to restore public support, board members may also lose their jobs over such conflicts; in this instance the mayor may remove board members. The competing groups in a school system often actively attempt to shape the resolution of these controversies.

DIRECTIONS FOR ROLE PLAYING

Roles

1. Nine members of the board of education
2. Superintendent of schools

3. President of the teachers' union
4. Representative from the Woodacres governing board
5. Administrator of the Woodacres subdistrict
6. Representative of the mayor
7. Officer of city parents' association
8. Officer of civil rights association

Procedures

The role playing occurs at a public hearing called by the board of education to consider what action should be taken to prevent a renewed teachers' strike. In an informal meeting following the public session the board decides what to do, based on the views it has heard. The following choices are to be considered:

1. Allow the subdistrict governing board to dismiss the ten teachers and to control its personnel decisions in the future.
2. Close the Woodacres schools and suspend the local governing board until the subdistrict agrees to take back the teachers. Enforce this action by cutting off all funds to the subdistrict, until an agreement is reached.
3. Same as the second choice; then after reaching an agreement, send observers into the subdistrict to ensure that the agreement is fulfilled.
4. Suspend the governing board and the administrator of the subdistrict.
5. Same as the fourth choice, then make the state the trustee of the subdistrict and require all observers to report to the state. Provide state supervision to ensure that right of the teachers in the whole district are not violated. If their rights are violated, the state can close the offending school.

The sequence of board of education hearings is as follows:

1. Public meeting
   a. Chairman of the board of education opens meeting and explains procedures.
   b. Statements of position from superintendent, union, local governing board, administrator, mayor, city parents' association, and civil rights association.
   c. Questions by the board of education members at any time during the statements.
   d. Chairman closes meeting.
2. Informal meeting
   a. Chairman asks for discussion from the board of education members and the superintendent.
   b. Chairman tries to get the board of education members to agree on a course of action, and at the end of the meeting he summarizes the decision reached.

The instructor assigns roles (number of people assigned to a given role will vary with class size) and establishes time limits appropriate to the class schedule. Each group of role players should meet briefly before the role playing starts, to plan its strategy.

Instructions for Roles

Each participant may elaborate on the facts presented to fill in gaps but may not change the facts as presented in this case.

1. Members of the board of education
   a. Chairman of the board of education
      (1) Serve as moderator of both the public and the informal meetings.
      (2) Open the public meeting by explaining the issue, the possible alternatives and the procedures to be followed so that all interested parties will have equal time to make their positions known.
      (3) Call on the various speakers in the order of the list of roles.
      (4) Be sure that they do not exceed the allotted time limits.
      (5) Accept questions from board of education members and moderate any exchanges between them and the speakers.
      (6) Conclude the meeting by thanking participants and explaining that the board of education will continue its deliberations in private sessions.
      (7) Act as chairman of the informal meeting, directing the deliberations about which option the board of education will follow.
      (8) Announce the decision of the board of education at the end of the meeting.
      (9) Ask questions or make statements at any point indicating your views as a Catholic Democrat.
   b. Other board of education members
      (1) React to the testimony by questions or statements, and try to persuade other members to support your position during the private meeting.
      (2) Develop your positions in light of the following information on the background of board of education members:
         (a) Catholic lawyer responsive to labor
         (b) Catholic lawyer
         (c) Protestant black foundation official
         (d) Protestant university official
         (e) Protestant lawyer active in civil rights organizations
         (f) Jewish businessman
         (g) Jewish woman active in parents' association, originally supported by liberal white groups and ghetto parents
         (h) Jewish labor official
2. Superintendent of schools. This dispute has a long, complicated history during which the Woodacres governing board has repeatedly tried to usurp authority from the board of education. It has refused to work through the regular channels and has rejected proposals that would long

ago have settled the controversy. The subdistrict governing board now makes charges that do not fit the facts. For example, it says that the ten teachers were dismissed only after requests to transfer them were refused. But the administrator of Woodacres never asked for the transfer of the ten teachers. If he had, the board of education would have arranged the transfer. It had transferred many other teachers from Woodacres and the other demonstration subdistricts. The behavior of the local governing board suggests that it has purposely pursued a collision course.

3. President of the teachers' union. Unless the board of education suspends the Woodacres governing board and administrator and returns all the teachers, many more teachers will be intimidated or fired. Subdistricts such as Woodacres have become the tool of extremist forces, which perpetuate segregation and politicize the schools. The results are lower standards, inequalities in the subdistricts, and inefficient duplication. No agreement made by the Woodacres governing board is reliable; it has repeatedly violated its promises to the superintendent. The mayor and the superintendent are not to be trusted either. They are much too willing to give in to the Woodacres people. Thus the union insists on the presence of its observers in the Woodacres schools to see that any agreement is actually implemented. These observers must also have the power to close a school where violations occur.

4. Representative from the Woodacres governing board. The board of education has done all it could to frustrate the wishes of the governing board. We took action against the ten teachers after all legitimate channels were blocked. If the board attempts to suspend us, we shall seek an injunction. We are a legal body. How can the needs of ten teachers take priority over the needs of the children in Woodacres? The Woodacres board represents the community and is responsive to the community's needs. The community must control its schools, and we refuse to be dictated to by the union or the board of education.

5. Administrator of the Woodacres subdistrict. I was hired by the local governing board and must follow its wishes. Many teachers sent to us by the board of education to replace teachers who left when the experiment started were incompetent. Requests to have certain teachers transferred were denied, and thus further requests were pointless because they too would have been denied.

6. Mayor's representative. The union should not cripple the entire school system because of problems in one school. The union is doing this to hurt the mayor, whose attempts to bring in outside negotiators have been rejected. If the board of education does not act soon, the mayor will have to act.

7. Officer of the city parents' association. Why have all the officials allowed the local governing board to defy the board of education's contract with the union? Such insubordination must not be permitted. The mayor and his appointees on the board of education are giving in to the demands of blacks for political reasons. None of the key figures in this controversy has children in the schools, so they are not suffering. We must bear the brunt of their political maneuvering.

8. Officer of the civil rights association. The union has purposely escalated the troubles at Woodacres to hurt legislation on decentralization, which

is pending at the state level. The teachers at the Woodacres schools were not fired; the district was merely carrying out a routine transfer. But the union wanted to discredit the idea of decentralization and thus has tried to make the Woodacres board seem irresponsible and to imply that such activities are inevitable under a decentralized system. As a result of the strike the union is actually gaining power over personnel matters rather than losing power.

QUESTIONS FOR DISCUSSION AFTER COMPLETION OF ROLE PLAYING

1. What factors shaped the decision of the board of education?
2. What effect will the decision of the board of education have on the union and the Woodacres governing board?
3. How does the decision of the board of education compare with the decisions reached by actual boards in similar situations?
4. What resources did each participant in the controversy have? For example, what factors helped the subdistrict governing board? How could each participant have achieved a more favorable outcome?
5. Why did each participant follow the strategy it did? For instance, why did the union strike in the entire school system over problems in one school? Why did the Woodacres governing board refuse to let the ten teachers back into the subdistrict?
6. Who runs the schools in this case? Is the power structure elitist or pluralist; that is, are the schools run by one small group, or are many groups involved? How much power do the professional educators have?
7. Who won the controversy described in this role playing case? Why?
8. To whom should the subdistrict school board be responsible—city government, parents, students, teachers, or the community?
9. Who should control education? An independent board of laymen? Professional educators? Elected officials? Students? Who is qualified to decide education policy?
10. Should the governing of school districts be decentralized? What powers should be given to subdistricts, and who should control them?
11. Can decentralization of school systems threaten the professional autonomy of teachers? Will subdistricts violate due process and academic freedom?
12. Should public employees have the right to strike, or should antistrike laws be maintained and strengthened?
13. What strategies are most effective in promoting educational reform? Why?
14. How did the class handle the role playing? How might the roles be performed differently? What might have been some of the artificialities in the role playing?
15. What were the class's reactions to role playing? What are the advantages and disadvantages for education?
16. How did the class handle the *discussion* of role playing? Comment on both the content and the process of the discussion.

proposed amendment to a state constitution

mass transit and air pollution control versus highways

10

SITUATION

In a populous, substantially urban state, long-term state bonds financed highway construction in the first two decades of the twentieth century. Paying the interest and principal on these bonds over a lengthy period of time (some bonds were not retired until 1965) was costly; and in some instances this expense doubled the ultimate cost of road building. To gain another means of highway financing and thus place less dependence on the costly bonding method, in 1923 the state legislature levied its first gasoline tax in the amount of two cents for each gallon. Half of the money went into a state highway fund to be employed exclusively for state highway repair and maintenance. The other half was allotted to local governments for local roads.

Since motorists make use of highways and roads in approximate proportion to their use of gasoline, the equitability of a gasoline tax was readily accepted and the gasoline pump promptly proved to be an inexpensive, convenient locale at which to collect this levy. The state gasoline tax was later raised, ultimately to more than double its original level, to pay also for new major highway and road construction. The increased revenue made it possible to proceed with the state highway program and most local road building projects on a pay-as-you-go basis.

During the years of economic hard times in the 1930s, many efforts were made to divert part of the state gasoline tax money from current highway construction and maintenance. A state ballot proposition in 1933 sought permission to use a portion of this tax revenue to pay for indebtedness incurred earlier for highway work. The voters turned down the proposal by a two-to-one margin. In this same period a rash of demands was made on the state legislature to allocate some of this money for nonhighway purposes, including old-age pensions and unemployment relief.

A reaction to these endeavors developed in the form of a proposed state constitutional amendment, which was presented to the people in 1938. Its objective was to restrict the use of the state gasoline tax, as well as motor vehicle registration and license fees, to highway construction and maintenance and the related purpose of enforcing traffic laws on these roads. The electorate decisively approved the proposed amendment by a resounding vote of almost two to one.

Almost twenty years passed before serious attempts were again made to tap the state gasoline tax money for different purposes. At this time, however, the legislature could not produce a change by altering an existing law; instead the voters would have to sanction a further amendment. That sanction failed to come in both 1958 and 1960, when proposals were devised to permit local governments to issue bonds for purposes other than roads to be paid from the gasoline tax. Several years later the state's attorney general ruled that the constitutional amendment of 1938 prevented the use of this tax money to pay general debt of the state or local governments even for highway purposes.

In the 1960s interest in doing away with restricting the state gasoline tax money solely to highway activities had gained considerable momentum. In 1969 a state constitutional revision commission recommended, by a decisive vote, sweeping changes in the gasoline tax section of the state constitution. It urged an amendment to allow four uses of the money in this tax fund: highway construction and maintenance and highway traffic regulation, which were the present two uses, plus plant and equipment expenditures for mass transit systems, and control of pollution caused by motor vehicles. (Construction of parking lots, a fifth use that the commission had approved earlier, was deleted by the commission's final vote of approval to send the recommendation on to the legislature.) The commission's action came after nearly a year of deliberation, during which 130 statements, many of them spirited, had been made to this body on the subject. The commission also urged that the proposal be assigned a separate place on the ballot so as not to jeopardize the chances for successful passage of less controversial amendments that it had proposed.

The many defenders and protesters of the measure then shifted their bitter fight to the state legislative halls. There the advocates had to gain at least a two-thirds vote of the total membership of each of the two legislative houses to have the proposed constitutional amendment placed before the voters. The contest over the measure in the legislature was hard fought and extensive, and many interest groups entered into the fray. The voters have a right to reevaluate their decision of 1938, when the state's population was only one-fourth its present total and motor vehicles merely one-twentieth as numerous as today, argued persons who wanted the proposal submitted as a state constitutional amendment. The public has twice upheld that decision, countered their opponents, and there is no reason to raise the question again. The proposal cleared one legislative house with the exact minimum necessary for passage and got through the other house with only one vote to spare.

The state legislature placed the proposed state constitutional amendment on the ballot in 1970. In its final form the proposition authorized the use of revenue from the state gasoline tax and motor vehicle fees for two additional purposes (beyond the previously authorized ones of highway construction and maintenance and traffic enforcement on such roads). The first involved constructing (if necessary), equipping, and bond financing mass transit systems (rail or bus, for instance); the second involved controlling environmental pollution caused by motor vehicles. No more than 25 percent of the state highway money generated in a county and up to the same percentage of state gasoline tax funds allotted to local governments for highway purposes could be spent on mass transit. This expenditure could be made, however, only after the voters in a county approved such a plan. On the other hand, the amendment specified no formula concerning expenditures for environmental pollution control; the state legislature would determine such a formula.

ISSUES

1. Is it discriminatory to utilize revenue generated by one type of transportation user, the motorist, for purposes other than highway construction and maintenance and traffic regulation, which are of immediate benefit to him?
2. Is the long-time segregation or earmarking of revenue from particular sources of income (for instance, the gasoline tax and motor vehicle fees) to finance a specific public activity (such as highway construction) sound public policy?
3. Should the phrase "related purpose" be narrowly or broadly defined in deciding what uses are appropriate for earmarked or segregated public money? A narrow interpretation of highway-related purpose would confine the employment of gasoline tax and motor vehicle fee money to highway construction and maintenance and traffic regulation. A broad

interpretation would include financial support for public transportation and air pollution control.

4. If revenue from particular income sources is to be segregated for special use, who should decide what related use is appropriate? The voters through amending the state constitution? The state legislature through state legislation?

BACKGROUND

Provisions in a state constitution are legally superior to state laws in the eyes of the courts; and if the two are in conflict, the judiciary will rule in favor of the constitution. Also, even in states where constitutions have been amended many times, a subject is still more difficult to change in a state constitution than in a state legislation because amending a state constitution involves at least two steps. One step is presentation of a proposal to the voters by action of the state legislature (sometimes similar actions at two successive annual or biennial sessions are required) or by petition from a substantial number of people (the latter, which is a type of initiative, is unavailable in some states). The other is subsequent sanction by the electorate.

Special interest groups primarily concerned about one government function, whether highways, education, public welfare, or another public activity, regularly seek to protect their favorite service by getting revenues earmarked or dedicated to it. This action assures a continuous flow of income for the function, which does not have to struggle each year or two for every dollar in competition with every other public service.

A minimum form of such protection is to obtain the passage of a state law that specifies setting aside certain money for the favored public activity. This procedure may be an adequate safeguard for a number of years, as was true in the gasoline tax diversion case that we are now considering. In time, other groups with another special interest will almost certainly want to see their preferred function included as a purpose of the earmarked revenue. They proceed to pressure the state legislature to make the protection less exclusive. Supporters of the already protected function then often seek to insulate their activity by taking it from the legislative arena into the more rarified atmosphere of the state constitution. The oil companies, road construction firms, automobile clubs, and other staunch highway proponents in the case under review acted in just this way.

Once the protection is written into the constitution, its supporters are in an easier position to defend. The antagonists who try to intrude usually find such protective walls harder to scale. In the case under consideration legislation served as a protective mantle for fifteen years, but the constitutional cocoon had existed for more than twice as long when the most recent election was held to do away with this exclusive province for highways.

DIRECTIONS FOR ROLE PLAYING

Roles

1. University or college professor or labor arbitrator to serve as moderator
2. Governor's press secretary
3. State senator
4. State league of women voters' representative
5. Officer, state chamber of commerce
6. Executive director, state association of municipalities
7. President, state taxpayers' association
8. Mass transit system official
9. Official, state automobile association
10. Member of Clean Air Now (CAN) organization
11. Oil company executive
12. Television studio audience
    For instance, staff member of a minority organization, spokesman for the trucking industry, member of a local civic league, member of a county governing board, city councilman, high school and college students, and other interested people

Procedures

The various role players take part in a television program (or programs) carried over a special statewide television network soon before the election on the proposed state constitutional amendment. The instructor assigns roles (number of people assigned to a given role varies with class size) and establishes time limits appropriate to the class schedule. Before the program, the moderator meets with the scheduled participants to work out the format and the aspects of the topic to be covered.

1. Format. They agree that the contending parties may make statements or ask questions of one another, or do both. They further agree that the studio audience may raise questions after the presentations.
2. Subjects Included. They decide that these phases of the subject will be considered in the following order (other aspects of the subject may be added or substituted by agreement of the players and the instructor):
   a. Decisions about use of existing state highway funds should be made partly at the local level or fully at the state level.
   b. Mass transit and air pollution are or are not highway-related purposes.

c. Highways need all the money they are receiving.
d. More mass transit will or will not produce overall transportation improvement.
e. Air pollution control should or should not be a part of this proposed state constitutional amendment.
3. Questions by studio audience. The role players and the instructor should determine the relative amounts of time to be given to each subject. Each participant in a subject area should be allowed approximately equal time.

Instructions for Roles

Each participant may elaborate on the facts presented to fill in gaps but may not change the facts as presented in the situation. Participants are expected to go beyond the wording of the statements included here. They may also convert some statements to questions.

1. Moderator
   a. Open the program by briefly introducing the topic for discussion.
   b. Keep the subject moving by making transitions, and when necessary insert a clarifying question or statement.
   c. Be aware of the allotted time and diplomatically stop anyone who is exceeding his time limit. Each viewpoint should be heard.
   d. Conclude by indicating the subjects that have been treated on the program and the specific question on which the electorate is being asked to cast votes.
   e. At the conclusion of the program (or programs), poll the class by secret ballot on the proposed state constitutional amendment, and announce the poll results.
2. Governor's press secretary: Subject a. Proponent of amendment. The governor of the state has long believed that decisions of this type should be vested in the people at the local level. Adoption of this proposed amendment means that the voters of a local community, in a separate election, will be able to decide whether they want a portion of the state gasoline and motor vehicle fee money to be allocated to mass transit in that area. Freedom of choice should be restored to the people. Every community around the state should be permitted to help devise the total transportation system most appropriate to its local needs, policies, values, and constituency. The electorate of a locality will not choose to exercise this option if the automobile is by itself largely meeting its transportation requirements successfully.
3. State senator: Subject a. Opponent of amendment. Highways are basic to the well-being of a state whose parts are interdependent; decisions about the use of state money presently devoted to highways constitute a matter of state policy, which should be made at the state level. Highways and expressways (freeways) are the leading elements in the total transportation system and the principal facilitators of interarea travel. To permit a diversion of an important part of their financing would be to allow a damaging, parochial intrusion into a critical state program.

4. State league of women voters' representative: Subject b. Proponent of amendment. The advocates of this proposal are not supporting indiscriminate forays against gasoline tax and motor vehicle fee revenue. Mass transit and air pollution control are as related to highway building and traffic regulation as the latter two original purposes of the constitutional section are related to one another. They are all highway-related purposes. Mass transit and smog have become major problems since the passage of the constitutional amendment in 1938. Their seriousness may be traced in large part to the rapid growth in the use of automobiles, and this expansion has been greatly facilitated by the segregation of so much state money for road building. Fairness and logic dictate that highway users should bear part of the cost of curing these problems.

5. Officer, state chamber of commerce: Subject b. Opponent of amendment. Where will the efforts to tap the state highway fund for other purposes end if this proposition is passed? In some people's minds the automobile is in many ways to blame for practically all our ills, and in such reasoning virtually every government activity is therefore a highway-related purpose. The basic objectives of the constitutional amendment of 1938—highway construction and maintenance and traffic regulation on such roads—are sound uses of this revenue and should continue to be the sole ones. Money needed for mass transit should be provided through the usual procedure of budget appropriations and not obtained by the devious maneuver of diverting part of the gasoline tax receipts and motor vehicle fee revenue.

6. Executive director, state association of municipalities: Subject c. Proponent of amendment. It is true that there are insufficient funds to provide for all the expressways, streets, and roads needed in the state, but this has always been true and will always be the case. It is also true that no segregated funds are available for mass transit or for environmental pollution caused by motor vehicles. The expressway system is highly congested at peak hours, and it is time to give more support to other methods of transportation. Likewise, the current smog control programs have been too little and too late, and new emergency approaches should be decided on and put into effect immediately. The essential ingredient for mass transit and smog control is money; the most readily available source is a portion of the revenue now going entirely to highways. Also, the state cannot qualify for federal rapid-transit funds unless it raises more money for such transportation. This ballot proposition will not raise taxes, as the opponents say it will; it will only permit more intelligent use of certain state money.

7. President, state taxpayers' association: Subject c. Opponent of amendment. Have you ever seen a proposal that may be more aptly termed "highway robbery"? Isn't there a complete lack of logic in the whole concept of taking money generated by highway use to support mass transit to reduce highway use, and thereby produce less money for mass transit? If this proposition were to pass and transit systems were successfully to lure many people from their automobiles, the people would be reducing the revenue they received from this source, which is based on motor vehicle usage. Moreover, raids on highway funds in other states have consistently damaged highway programs. If money is taken from one part of the state's transportation system to support another part, taxes will

have to increase. The simple truth is that people will continue to need the roads, and money will have to be found to replace the diverted funds. Increased taxes will hurt people of moderate incomes the most.

8. Mass transit system official: Subject d. Proponent of amendment. We need a balanced system of transportation, involving improved mass transit, to make the total transportation output better. The vast amount of money the state is spending on urban expressways is not buying a measurably improved level of service. The commuting time by automobile is not declining, and the annual toll of traffic fatalities continues to rise. The related social costs attributed to smog and congestion are also continuing to increase. We need to reorder the transportation priorities and furnish substantial aid, for the first time, to mass transit, which will improve travel time and reduce air pollution and congestion. If successful transit systems are installed, fewer highways and expressways will be necessary.

9. Official, state automobile association: Subject d. Opponent of amendment. Surveys confirm that as a means of transportation, at any time—except for business trips of more than 500 miles—most residents of this state prefer to use their automobiles. Investment of a great amount of money in mass transit is indeed unwise because given a choice most people would select the personalized transportation afforded by a private car. What is the evidence that more and better mass transit systems will siphon off enough traffic to solve either the smog or the congestion problem or·be of noticeable benefit to commuters electing to remain on the expressway system? In addition too much emphasis is being placed in this campaign on the movement of people. An expanding highway network is required to accommodate the ever-increasing growth of commerce moved by trucks.

10. Member of Clean Air Now (CAN) organization: Subject e. Proponent of amendment. Motor vehicle users contribute significantly to air pollution and consequently should contribute to its elimination. The dirty brown clouds hanging over the urban areas and endangering the health and welfare of their people must be wiped out. The producers of fuel also have a great responsibility. Evaporation of gasoline is one of the worst sources of smog, and the underground gasoline tanks at every service station emit fumes into the air.

11. Oil company executive: Subject f. Opponent of amendment. The smog issue is a red herring raised by supporters of this proposition to distract attention from the lack of public enthusiasm for the real purpose of the proposal and to give the measure some popular appeal. That purpose is to aid deteriorating mass transit operations. Ample money can be raised for smog abatement under present state law without tampering with the safeguards to highways built into the current constitutional section.

12. Television studio audience—sample of possible comments
   a. Staff member of minority organization. The poor, made up mostly of racial and ethnic minorities and the elderly, cannot afford automobile transportation to get to jobs or places of recreation. Their only alternative is inadequate bus service. How and when are we going to acquire sufficient mass transit so that we can break out of our walled-in communities?
   b. Representative of conservation organization. If this proposition is de-

feated, will the state highway department's equipment move on and on until most of the state will be paved over with concrete and asphalt?

c. Spokesman for trucking industry. If this proposed constitutional amendment passes, will the highway and expressway program in this state be destroyed? If not destroyed, seriously delayed?

d. Member of a local civic league. Many of my friends and I favor better air pollution control and more highways and expressways, but we are dubious about the practical value of improved mass transit. Is there any way to vote for smog control and against transit at the election on this issue?

QUESTIONS FOR DISCUSSION AFTER COMPLETION OF ROLE PLAYING

1. What was the result of the class vote taken on the proposed constitutional amendment?

2. What do you feel were the most important reasons for the approval or disapproval of the proposal by the class?

3. Do you believe that the vote of an actual state electorate was favorable or unfavorable? Why?

4. What are some reasons why the class decision and the actual decision might be the same or in opposition?

5. Was the program persuasive in your reaching a conclusion about how to vote?

6. If the program was persuasive, how was it so?

7. If the program was not persuasive, how did you reach your decision about the proposition?

8. Did the organizational affiliation of any or many of the participants affect your decision? Why?

9. Why did the various participants take the position they did? Did any of them think they represented the public interest? Which actually did? How can the public interest be discovered?

10. Is a television program of this type an effective means of communicating information about public issues of this kind?

11. How did the class handle the role playing? How might the roles be performed differently? What might have been some artificialities in the role playing?

12. What were the class's reactions to role playing? What are the advantages and disadvantages for education?

13. How did the class handle the *discussion* of role playing? Comment on both the content and the process of the discussion. Did the class listen to various points of view? How did it react to differing opinions expressed in the discussion after the role playing? Did the class members consider other opinions or reject them? Did they help clarify the comments of various participants, by asking questions? Did class members help summarize and direct the discussion?

a state legislative hearing
on a proposed metropolitan
government

11

The metropolitan area, much of which is traversed by a river and its tributaries, contains more than 100,000 inhabitants and stretches over two counties in the same state (or if in New England, where such areas are defined differently, it includes a major city and a number of adjacent towns). The central city and the suburbs (the latter encompassing all the metropolis except the central city) are both still growing in population; but the suburban areas, especially those in the outlying sectors, are expanding much faster. The suburban population is now greater than that of the central city. The migration of many people, mostly black and other minority individuals and families, from rural land has produced a substantial portion of the population growth.

Many newcomers have of necessity settled in older, often segregated and decaying portions of the central city, where most of the low-income housing is to be found. At the same time a considerable number of prosperous white residents of the metropolis have moved from the central city to new suburban developments. Increasingly the central city has become the home of the poor, the minorities, and the elderly, whereas the suburbs have become the places of residence of more and more well-to-do whites. The social dichotomy is far from complete, however, as many blue-collar white workers and some minority and poor people reside in certain suburbs. Some suburban housing was poorly constructed and is deteriorating rapidly.

The metropolitan area is a sizable industrial and commercial center, with its large factories, bank and other financial institution headquarters, and wholesale trade outlets located almost without exception in the central city. Its central business district is deteriorating, although some redevelopment is under way there. The suburbs are mainly residential; but regional shopping centers, often featuring large branches of downtown department stores and supermarkets, are appearing more frequently in suburban locales.

Government in this metropolitan area is complex, with most local units of small territorial size. Two county governments, which together cover the entire metropolitan territory and are about equal in area, have not undergone major administrative reorganizations but instead still have many independently elected department heads. Moreover the continuing severe limitations in financial ability serves as a constraint on their extensive expansion into new services. Thirty-five municipalities, ranging greatly in area, financial resources, and functions, are active; their number has increased by eight in the last decade.

The central city government, which is also the county seat, is by far the largest in each of the aforementioned categories; nevertheless, it embraces less than one-tenth of the metropolitan area. It has a mayor–council form of government, with a strong mayor who can make numerous patronage appointments because the city has only a partial formal merit system. Its council meets frequently, and council service is the principal occupation of most of its councilmen. Government officials of the central city have been trying to work out solutions to some of the area's common problems; however, many private leaders living in the suburbs but owning or managing businesses in the central city are suspicious of and dislike the city's official leadership and are reluctant to collaborate.

Many suburbs have employed city (or town) managers, and their bureaucracies usually have a high degree of professionalism. Their councils generally meet only once or twice a month, and all their councilmen spend a limited amount of time on the job. Some suburbs have entered into cooperative agreements, most notably for sewage disposal and other facilities requiring large capital money outlays and extended negotiations. These agreements have almost always been with suburbs of comparable socioeconomic characteristics rather than with the central city or dissimilar suburbs.

School districts are more numerous than municipalities in the metropolis (except in New England, where they are fewer in number). Many districts do not have identical boundaries with municipalities, the result of many school leaders' desire to keep education independent of general local governments and thus out of local politics (which is not the same as school politics). Some school districts in this area provide only the elementary grades of education, and in each such instance three or more of these units are within the territorial limits of another district supplying the high school educational grades. Other school districts offer both elementary and high school levels and sometimes even two years of community college work. All school districts have little to do with the general local units (except for filing reports with the county superintendent of schools). Their relations with the state government are much more regular.

Nonschool special districts are even more abundant than school districts in this urban complex. Most nonschool districts are small in territorial size and limited in the range of their activities, and they operate in suburban sections outside municipalities (that is, in unincorporated areas). There they provide such services as water, fire protection, sewage disposal, and garbage collection. In contrast, two types of special districts are sizable, although neither is employed on a metropolitan-wide basis. An air pollution control district, which is coterminous with the county boundaries, operates on a countrywide basis in each of the two counties in the metropolis. Five mass transit districts, three in the more populous county (which contains the central city) and two in the other, are active. Their main effort is the provision of bus service, although one district is developing plans for a limited rapid transit rail system.

A metropolitan council of governments is also functioning. Although it has member governments throughout the metropolitan area, it is not a metropolitan government. Instead its membership is voluntary and its activities, including the preparation of studies of metropolitan problems with recommendations and the development of a general regional plan, are advisory. It has neither mandatory financing nor enforcement power. The national government has designated the metropolitan council as the review agency to comment on the applications of general local units in the area for many kinds of federal grants with respect to the extent of their consistency with the general regional plan devised by the metropolitan council.

The state and national governments play important roles in the development of this metropolis. Through legislative and voter action, the state largely determines the form and much of the activity of the local units. In recent years the state government has been enlarging its financial assistance for particular metropolian programs and has been providing more direct services, as in the water and park and recreation fields, to metropolises. To an even greater extent than the state, the national government recently has become a bigger supplier of funds to this area, especially in such fields as airport, mass transit, highways, hospitals, urban renewal, and sewage treatment.

Serious metropolitan problems are present in this urban area. Despite the existence in both counties of air quality programs and state-mandated minimum standards, the inadequacy of one county's controls, greatly weakened by influential industrial firms, largely negates the adequate regulations in the other. A second aspect of damage to the environment is water pollution, which centers in the area's major river and tributary streams; the river and streams pass through many different governments that have allowed varying practices and imposed differing rules. Under authority vested in him by congressional act, the Secretary of the Interior called a conference of the many affected parties and threatened to start court action if satisfactory solutions could not be agreed on. Both the conference and the threatened court action were time-consuming efforts. Such agreements were made and implemented, but later two parties slipped back to a substandard level, and informal efforts are now under way to rectify the deficiencies.

Solid waste disposal is a third environment-related metropolitan weakness. Both counties, all cities, and many special districts in the metropolis separately decide how to dispose of solid waste. Some of their methods are insufficient and thus contribute to air pollution. Moreover, flies produced by inadequate disposal can make flights up to twenty miles and are therefore capable of detrimentally affecting the health of people in other parts of the metropolitan area. Also, most of the municipalities are unable to absorb their waste and must arrange for disposal outside their boundaries.

Mass transit and airport transportation are further metropolitan difficulties. The five operating transit systems provide slow instead of rapid service, their schedules are not synchronized, and in some instances they unnecessarily duplicate service. They do not operate, in total, throughout the metropolitan area, thereby giving only fragmentary service. Six different governments manage the airport facilities in the two-county area. The airport traffic volume is heavily concentrated in one airport, with resultant high levels of noise and accident hazards, even though an important portion of the traffic could be appropriately reassigned to the lesser-used air facilities. In addition, no existing government in the area wants to assume the extensive financial obligation incurred in building a regional airport, a facility that would promote the economic well-being of the metropolis.

As the area has grown in population total and density, open space of sizable proportions, including regional park and recreational sites, has become more difficult to acquire and retain. Once land usable for these purposes has been swallowed up by urban development, it has become too costly to regain. Few of the area's governments are sufficiently large in territory and financial resources to permit them to purchase large-scale open space, which contributes significantly to the quality of urban living. And none of these governments has shown a willingness to do so.

The metropolitan council of governments has undertaken metropolitan planning, but implementation of specific elements of the general areawide plan depends on positive, individual action by a large number of separate local units. Because such implementation has seldom occurred, the elements of the areawide plan largely have remained dust-gathering studies.

Racial and ethnic minority problems have had a long history in the metropolitan area; and tensions have periodically increased, most notably in the mid- and late 1960s. Some potentially major disturbances have been stifled from time to time, but no riot has developed. The principal and persistent grievances are the insufficient supply of adequate low- and middle-income housing and jobs, and police treatment of minorities.

The metropolitan area is thus faced with increasingly serious problems, which existing local government units are unable to handle. In response to pressures created by this situation the members of a state legislative committee have studied the needs of this metropolitan area and have drafted a bill providing for a metropolitan government there. After a public hearing by the legislative committee, the committee will present the bill, possibly modified, to the legislature.

The principal features of the bill are:

1. A metropolitan multipurpose district superimposed on all local governments in the area will be the form of the areawide government.
2. Its territorial jurisdiction will embrace the entire two-county metropolitan area.
3. Its functions, largely derived by reassignment from existing counties, municipalities, and special districts, will be:
   a. air quality control
   b. water pollution control
   c. solid waste disposal
   d. development and operation of airports of more than local significance and rapid mass transit facilities
   e. acquisition, development, and management of open space, including regional park and recreational areas
   f. metropolitan plans prepared and adopted by the metropolitan government, which is empowered to require local plans to adhere closely to the metropolitan plans.
4. Its financial authority will consist of property and income taxation, ser-

vice charges, revenue and general obligation bonds, and federal and state grants and other forms of financial assistance.

5. The metropolitan governing board will be composed of thirty-five members, twenty of whom will be directly elected for four-year terms from single-member electoral districts and fifteen of whom will be elected local officials chosen annually by their associates. All governing board members will represent as nearly equal numbers of people as possible.

6. The chief executive of the metropolitan government, who is to be the administrative head and a policy leader, will be directly elected on an areawide basis for a four-year term. He will prepare the annual budget, exercise the veto, and present policy messages to the metropolitan governing board and to the people, including an annual report on the state of the metropolis.

7. This metropolitan government proposal will go into effect ninety days after its passage by the state legislature. The metropolitan government may subsequently be revised or abolished by state legislative action.

ISSUES

1. Is a metropolitan government the best way of solving the metropolitan problems of this area?

2. If so, is the type of metropolitan government proposed the best one for this area? What kinds of advantages and disadvantages will result for which groups?

3. Are the proposed boundaries proper, too large, or too small?

4. Are all the functions appropriate to this government? Are some highly relevant functions missing?

5. Is its financing authority, particularly its taxing power, equitable?

6. Will the method of constituting the governing body provide sufficient accountability and responsiveness to the metropolitan public?

7. Is it undemocratic to permit this metropolitan government to be organized without first submitting the question to the voters of the metropolitan area?

BACKGROUND

Until the 1920s the government pattern of this metropolis was relatively simple. It consisted of one county; the present central city, which was dominant; eight small suburban municipalities, some close to the big urban center but others scattered throughout the county; and a few school and nonschool special districts. Until then the major city was largely able to keep pace with growth because the council could exercise the unilateral right, conferred by state law, to annex adjacent unincorporated land (territory beyond the boundaries of this municipality), which it did regularly, usually as that land was becoming urban.

The situation then changed drastically. Expanding use of the automobile made it possible to work in locations much farther from places of residence. New municipalities and special districts sprouted in this county, through employment of continued easy state formation laws, and many unincorporated urban areas cropped up. About the same time a coalition of suburban and rural members of the state legislature changed the state municipal annexation law to require a separate vote of approval by the residents of an area adjacent to a municipality (or petitions signed by persons in such an area, who owned more than half the property being annexed). Such sanction often was not forthcoming in the years ahead. No longer was the overwhelming proportion of development in this metropolis within a single municipality. No longer was a unified means at hand for dealing with urban problems. Now another method of unification or coordination would need to be used.

In the next two decades the number of people and governments continued to increase, as did the quantity of problems common to the central city and the incorporated and unincorporated suburbs in the county. Area leaders, primarily government officials and civic figures of the central city, sponsored a research study of these problems. Its main conclusion was that consolidation of the county government, the central city, and the suburban municipalities into a single unit (city–county consolidation) would establish an effective instrumentality for dealing with important metropolitan needs. These leaders then persuaded the state legislature to pass legislation permitting the formation of a consolidated city–county government in this metropolis. The law provided that to become operative the proposal had to attain dual popular majorities—one in the central city, the other in the rest of the county. The proposition received a decisive majority in the city. It lost even more resoundingly in the county, where the opponents argued that under this proposal the suburbs would be gobbled up by the central city, which still had about three-fifths of the metropolitan population.

As the next thirty years passed, the population of the area grew and overflowed into a second county, governments proliferated in both counties (except for school districts, which consolidated into a smaller number), and mutual problems became more acute and increasingly inter-county. During this period area leaders, again predominantly central city residents, pushed for another kind of comprehensive metropolitan reform in the original county. This time they got the state constitution amended to allow a local charter board to draw up a federated or two-level metropolitan government system. Like the preceding reform, this new charter had to obtain popular majorities in the county, both inside and outside the central city. Under this proposed charter, a metropolitan government would have absorbed the existing county government and would have been given certain areawide functions (for instance, the power to develop and operate a rapid mass transit system), which the county did not possess. All municipalities in the county would have countinued to exist, with slightly reduced powers and direct representation on the metropolitan governing board.

The federation charter received a majority of the votes in the central city (but a smaller proportion than had been acquired for the earlier consolidation plan), but it failed to garner a majority in the remainder of the county, even though the margin of defeat there was less than had been the case for city–county consolidation. Opposition came from two major sources: individuals and groups who felt the proposed change was too moderate in either a functional or a geographical sense (the metropolitan area was now intercounty) and those who believed the reform was too radical. Proponents argued in vain that the charter was a halfway house that could be altered in either direction, depending on what experience revealed. (However, to make the federation subsequently intercounty would have required a further amendment to the state constitution.)

In later years the government pattern has remained fairly stationary although the general trend has been toward greater government proliferation and complexity. Problems, when dealt with at all, have been treated on an individual and usually fragmentary basis. Two or more suburban municipalities have made various service agreements with one another, usually of minor importance. Following a long tradition, school districts purposely have scant contacts with municipal and county governments. Air pollution control and mass transit districts have been organized, but each covers only a limited portion of the metropolis and generally operate ineffectively. A metropolitan council of governments, which is an areawide advisory planning group, has been established. It was formed chiefly through stimulation by the national government, which provided financial assistance and required each metropolitan area to have an official areawide planning agency to which many types of federal grant applications by the local government of the area would have to be sent for comment.

DIRECTIONS FOR ROLE PLAYING

Roles

All the role players, except some of the state legislators, are from the metropolitan area for which the metropolitan government bill is proposed, unless otherwise indicated.

1. Senator A, chairman of legislative committee (extremely enthusiastic about the bill)
2. Representative A, committee member (supportive of all aspects of the proposal)
3. Senator B, committee member (supportive but has a cautious manner)
4. Representative B, committee member (generally supportive but has several reservations about the bill)
5. Senator C, committee member (completely opposed to the bill)
6. Central city mayor
7. President, suburban improvement association
8. Retired director, civic reform league
9. Suburban city manager
10. Regional planner
11. Mass transit executive
12. President, human relations commission
13. Environmentalist
14. Member, suburban taxpayers' association
15. Officer, league of women voters
16. Officer, minority organization
17. Suburban city councilman
18. President, state association of municipalities
19. President, private regional planning association

Procedures

This is a public hearing by a joint state legislative committee on a metropolitan government bill, which it has drafted, to see whether any modifications are needed before its submission to the legislature. The hearing is being held in the largest city in the metropolitan area where the new government would be established. Notice of the hearing was sent out to the mass media and possibly interested organizations a month ago; and persons were asked to make their desire to testify known, in writing, to the committee's executive secretary at least one week in advance of the scheduled date. The instructor assigns roles and establishes appropriate time limits.

Format. Scheduled witnesses come forward, in the order listed in the following instructions for roles, to testify on the committee's bill. Each witness supports or opposes the proposal, usually because of some particular provision. Any of the five legislative committee members may ask questions of any witness. The types of questions they pose and of whom they ask them depend on the respective attitudes of each state legislator toward the bill [see 1 through 5 above].

Instructions for Roles

Each participant may elaborate on the facts presented to fill in gaps but may not change the facts as presented in the situation.

1. Chairman of legislative committee. Call the meeting of the committee to order. State that this is a public hearing on the committee's bill to create a metropolitan government for a specific two-county area. Say copies of the bill have been distributed in advance so that participants in this meeting would have the opportunity to study its provisions beforehand. Have the committee's executive secretary pass out additional copies to persons in attendance who need them. Introduce the other four committee members (whose titles vary depending on the state in which the hearing is being held). Introduce each witness by name and title as he or she comes to the chair adjoining the committee table, to testify. At the end of the hearing, poll the class by secret ballot on approval or disapproval of the bill, and announce the poll results.

2. Central city mayor. Commend the legislative committee for the excellence of its proposal and announce your complete support for it. Point to the long history of unsuccessful reform efforts of a more comprehensive nature in the metropolis as its areawide problems grew in number and intensity. (Materals in Background and Situation, above, will be useful.) Praise this proposal for being tailor-made to the needs of this metropolis.

3. President, suburban improvement association. A powerful metropolitan government is unnecessary in this metropolitan area. We already have metropolitan governments in the form of air pollution and mass transit agencies, and no positive purpose will be served by merging them into a larger entity. The private citizens and public officials of this metropolis can solve its mutual problems through cooperative means, which include the voluntary metropolitan council of governments. We already have too much government in the metropolis.

4. Retired director, civic reform league. The proposal is all right as far as it goes, but it does not go far enough. We have too many local governments in the metropolis as is. Some are simply tax shelters formed by industry to avoid contributing a just share to financing services over a broader area. Other, poor localities have never been able to finance adequate levels of local services. A two-level system of government for the metropolitan area is satisfactory, but both levels must be adequate. Such is not the situation with the local level in this instance.

5. Suburban city manager. Although the functions suggested for this metropolitan government are of more than local impact, they do not all have effects throughout the two-county area, which is proposed as the boundaries. Therefore, I recommend that this government be given authority to set up one or more service subareas within its boundaries for financing particular services not of benefit on a metropolitanwide basis.

6. Regional planner. The proposed boundaries are too restricted for at least two functions—air and water quality control—prescribed for the new government. A bicounty scope for these two geographically extensive

problems would be little better than the one county territorial limits of the air pollution control district.

7. Mass transit executive. Control over the construction and location of new and improved highways in the metropolis simply has to be assigned to this metropolitan government. Highways and mass transit must be coordinated if the area is going to have an adequate transportation system. Lack of such coordination in the past is an important reason why the current system is woefully insufficient.

8. President, human relations commission. The proposal does not touch on two of the area's greatest problems: better law enforcement and improved low-income housing. We realize that the legislative committee is trying to establish a foundation that can be built on over the years. But we feel the foundation will indeed be shaky if these two problems are not included. There is too much discriminatory law enforcement in this metropolis, and our hope is to get a well-trained, nonracist metropolitan police force. Also, low-income housing must be viewed as a metropolitan problem financed as an areawide function; no individual municipality actively seeks to house such developments because of the low amount of public revenue they produce.

9. Environmentalist. Only a metropolitan government can deal properly with the problem of open space, which is disappearing rapidly from most communities in the metropolitan area. In addition most localities can no longer handle the cost of sizable amounts of land for open space. An areawide government with sufficient financing authority is the only hope.

10. Member, suburban taxpayers' association. The level of combined property taxation by the different local governments levying such taxes in the metropolitan area is already excessive. If this proposed new government makes substantial use of its property-taxing power, the confiscation of private property may be near. Home ownership is a foundation of American society; everything possible should be done to preserve it. On behalf of our association, I strongly urge the elimination of the power to tax property from the authority of this metropolitan agency.

11. Officer, league of women voters. The proposed financial powers of the metropolitan unit are sound and necessary. Some of the service functions may not be entirely self-supporting—for instance, rapid mass transit and open space—and therefore would have to be financed in part through property taxation.

12. Officer, minority organization. We want the governing body to consist entirely of persons directly elected to it by the voters. All or almost all of the fifteen local officials to serve on the governing board by appointment of their colleagues will probably be white. Also, people appointed to boards tend to be less accountable. We have struggled too long to increase our representational strength to sacrifice it in a combined direct–indirect scheme.

13. Suburban city councilman. The mixed appointed-elected system is satisfactory, although my preference and that of many other suburban officials is for an appointed scheme entirely. Continuing coordination and cooperation between the proposed metropolitan government and the local governments are absolute necessities if this plan of reform is to succeed. One of the best ways to guarantee such coordination and cooperation is

to have certain governing board members of the local units also serve as governing body members of the metropolitan government. Consequently the inclusion of a substantial number of local elected officials on the metropolitan council is a basic provision of the legislative bill.

14. President, state association of municipalities. We object strenuously to that feature of the proposed bill that allows the state legislature to put the plan into operation without a popular vote in the metropolitan area. Such a provision is coercive and antidemocratic. Every municipality in the metropolitan area was formed by popular vote. A similar procedure should be followed in setting up a powerful metropolitan government.

15. President, private regional planning association. Establishing this metropolitan unit by action of the state legislature is sound public policy. The state is the reservoir of all local government powers, and the state legislature is justified in acting in the present situation. Furthermore some of the problems of this metropolis have a statewide impact, and a proper metropolitan organization is thus appropriately a matter for state legislative attention.

QUESTIONS FOR DISCUSSION AFTER COMPLETION OF ROLE PLAYING

1. What was the result of the class vote taken on the proposed metropolitan government bill?
2. What do you feel were the most important reasons for the approval or disapproval of the bill by the class?
3. If the class rejected the bill, do you feel certain amendments to the original proposal would have changed defeat to victory?
4. Was the hearing persuasive in your reaching a conclusion about how to vote?
5. If the hearing was persuasive, how was it so?
6. If the hearing was not persuasive, how did you reach your decision about the proposed bill?
7. Did the organizational affiliation of any or many of the witnesses affect your decision? Why?
8. Is a legislative hearing an efficient way of gaining representative reactions to a proposal?
9. What effect might the hearing have on the legislators' opinions? On the draft of the metropolitan government bill?
10. Why did the various participants take the positions they did? Did any of them think they represented the public interest? Which actually did? How can the public interest be discovered?
11. How did the class handle the role playing? How might the roles be performed differently? What might have been some artificialities in the role playing?
12. What were the class's reactions to role playing? What are the advantages and disadvantages for education?

13. How did the class handle the *discussion* of role playing? Comment on both the content and the process of the discussion. Did the class listen to the various points of view? How did it react to differing opinions expressed in the discussion after the role playing? Did the class members consider other opinions or reject them? Did they help clarify the comments of various participants by asking questions? Did class members help summarize and direct the discussion?

bibliography

INTRODUCTION TO PARTICIPATION (CHAPTER 1)

ALINSKY, SAUL D. *Reveille for Radicals.* New York: Random House, 1969.

COOK, TERRENCE, and PATRICK MORGAN. *Participatory Democracy.* San Francisco: Canfield Press, 1971.

COX, FRED. *Strategies of Community Organization.* Itasca, Ill.: F. E. Peacock Publishers, 1970.

KAUFMAN, HERBERT. "Administrative Decentralization and Political Power." *Public Administration Review,* XXIX (January/February 1969), 3–14.

LANE, ROBERT. *Political Life.* New York: The Free Press, 1959.

LOWI, THEODORE. *The End of Liberalism.* New York: W. W. Norton, 1969.

LYNCH, THOMAS D., ed. "Symposium on Neighborhoods and Citizen Involvement," *Public Administration Review,* XXXII (May/June 1972), 189–223.

MARSHALL, DALE ROGERS. "Who Participates in What?" *Urban Affairs Quarterly,* IV (December 1968), 201–224.

MILBRATH, LESTER. *Political Participation.* Chicago: Rand McNally, 1965.

MOGULOF, MELVIN. *Citizen Participation.* Washington, D.C.: Urban Institute, 1970.

NADER, RALPH, and DONALD ROSS. *Action for a Change.* New York: Grossman Publishers, 1971.

THE ORGANIZER'S MANUAL COLLECTIVE. *The Organizer's Manual.* New York: Bantam Books, 1971.

TOCQUEVILLE, ALEXIS DE. *Democracy in America,* vols. I and II. New York: Alfred A. Knopf, 1946.

Introduction to Field Work (Chapters 2–6)

Almond, Gabriel, and Sydney Verba. *The Civic Culture.* Boston: Little, Brown, 1965.

Andreano, Ralph, Evan Farber, and Sabron Reynolds. *The Student Economist's Handbook.* Cambridge, Mass.: Schenkman Publishing, 1967.

Backstrom, Charles H., and Gerald Hursh. *Survey Research.* Evanston, Ill.: Northwestern University Press, 1963.

Bart, Pauline, and Linda Frankel. *The Student Sociologist's Handbook.* Cambridge, Mass., Schenkman Publishing, 1971.

Barzun, Jacques. *On Writing, Editing, and Publishing.* Chicago: University of Chicago Press, 1971.

Barzun, Jacques, and Henry Graff. *The Modern Researcher.* New York: Harcourt Brace Jovanovich, 1970.

Benson, Oliver. *Political Science Laboratory.* Columbus, Ohio: Charles E. Merrill, 1969.

Blau, Peter. *The Dynamics of Bureaucracy.* Chicago: University of Chicago Press, 1963.

Bollens, John C., ed. *Exploring the Metropolitan Community.* Berkeley and Los Angeles: University of California Press, 1961.

Broom, Leonard, and Philip Selznick. *Sociology.* New York: Harper and Row, 1963.

Campbell, Angus, Philip E. Converse, Warren E. Miller, and Donald E. Stokes. *The American Voter.* New York: John Wiley and Sons, 1960.

Crozier, Michel. *The Bureaucratic Phenomenon.* Chicago: University of Chicago Press, 1964.

Dahl, Robert. *Who Governs: Democracy and Power in an American City.* New Haven, Conn.: Yale University Press, 1961.

Deutsch, Morton, and Mary Collins. *Interracial Housing: A Psychological Evaluation of a Social Experiment.* Minneapolis: University of Minnesota Press, 1951.

Festinger, Leon, and Daniel Katz. *Research Methods in the Behavioral Sciences.* New York: Holt, Rinehart and Winston, 1953.

Gans, Herbert J. *The Urban Villagers.* New York: The Free Press, 1962.

Goffman, Erving. *Asylums.* Chicago: Aldine Publishing, 1962.

Goode, William J., and Paul K. Hatt. *Methods in Social Research.* New York: McGraw-Hill, 1952.

Gouldner, Alvin. *Patterns of Industrial Bureaucracy.* New York: The Free Press, 1954.

Gowers, Ernest. *Complete Plain Words.* Baltimore: Penguin Books, 1962.

Greer, Scott. *Urban Renewal and American Cities.* Indianapolis: Bobbs-Merrill, 1965.

Hammond, Phillip E., ed. *Sociologists at Work: Essays on the Craft of Social Research.* New York: Basic Books, 1964.

HOLLINGSHEAD, AUGUST B., and FREDERICK C. REDLICH. *Social Class and Mental Illness.* New York: John Wiley and Sons, 1958.

HOMANS, GEORGE C. *The Human Group.* New York: Harcourt Brace Jovanovich, 1950.

HOSELITZ, BERT F., ed. *A Reader's Guide to the Social Sciences.* New York: The Free Press, 1970.

HUDSON, BARBARA J., and ROBERT McDONALD. *Metropolitan Communities, A Bibliography Supplement: 1958–1964.* Chicago: Public Administration Service, 1967.

HUNTER, FLOYD. *Community Power Structure.* Chapel Hill: University of North Carolina Press, 1953.

HURT, PEYTON. *Bibliography and Footnotes: A Style Manual for College and University Students.* Berkeley: University of California Press, 1963.

HYMAN, HERBERT. *Survey Design and Analysis.* New York: The Free Press, 1955.

JOHNSON, SHEILA. *Idle Haven.* Berkeley and Los Angeles: University of California Press, 1971.

KAPLAN, ABRAHAM. *The Conduct of Inquiry: Methodology for Behavioral Science.* San Francisco: Chandler Publishing, 1965.

KATZ, ELIHU, and PAUL LAZARSFELD. *Personal Influence.* New York: The Free Press, 1955.

KENISTON, KENNETH. *Young Radicals.* New York: Harcourt Brace Jovanovich, 1968.

KENNEDY, JOHN F. *Why England Slept.* New York: W. Funk, 1940.

KINSEY, ALFRED C., WARDELL POMEROY, and CLYDE E. MARTIN. *Sexual Behavior in the Human Male.* Philadelphia: W. B. Saunders, 1948.

LANE, ROBERT. *Political Ideology.* New York: The Free Press, 1962.

LEWIS, ANTHONY. *Gideon's Trumpet.* New York: Vintage Books, 1964.

LEWIS, OSCAR. *The Children of Sanchez.* New York: New American Library, 1961.

LIEBOW, ELLIOT. *Tally's Corner.* Boston: Little, Brown, 1967.

LIPSET, SEYMOUR, MARTIN TROW, and JAMES COLEMAN. *Union Democracy.* Garden City: N.Y.: Doubleday, 1956.

MADGE, JOHN. *The Tools of Social Science.* Garden City, N.Y.: Doubleday, 1965.

MERRITT, RICHARD, and GLORIA J. PYSZKA. *The Student Political Scientist's Handbook.* Cambridge, Mass.: Schenkman Publishing, 1969.

MOYNIHAN, DANIEL P. "Statement on Report of World Social Situation in Committee III, United Nations." New York: United Nations, October 7, 1971 (mimeo.).

PARTEN, MILDRED. *Surveys, Polls, and Samples.* New York: Harper and Brothers, 1950.

ROURKE, FRANCIS. *Bureaucracy, Politics, and Public Policy.* Boston: Little, Brown, 1969.

SARBIN, THEODORE, and WILLIAM COLE. *The Student Psychologist's Handbook.* Cambridge, Mass.: Schenkman Publishing, 1969.

SCHATTSCHNEIDER, E. E., and VICTOR JONES. *Local Political Surveys*. New York: Holt, Rinehart and Winston, 1962.

SCOBLE, HARRY. *Ideology and Electoral Action*. San Francisco: Chandler Publishing, 1967.

SCOBLE, HARRY, and STANLEY BACHRACK. "Mailed Questionnaires: Controlled Reduction of Nonresponse," *Public Opinion Quarterly*, XXXI (Summer 1967), 265–71.

SELLTIZ, CLAIRE, MARIE JAHODA, MORTON DEUTSCH, and STUART COOK. *Research Methods in Social Relations*, rev. ed. New York: Holt, Rinehart, and Winston, 1963.

SELZNICK, PHILIP. *TVA and the Grass Roots*. Berkeley: University of California Press, 1949.

SILLS, DAVID L., ed. *International Encyclopedia of the Social Sciences*. New York: The Free Press, 1968.

SKILLIN, MARJORIE E., ROBERT M. GAY, and others. *Words into Type*, rev. ed. New York: Appleton-Century-Crofts, 1964.

STOUFFER, SAMUEL, and others. *The American Soldier*. Princeton, N.J.: Princeton University Press, 1949.

STRUNK, WILLIAM S., JR., and E. B. WHITE. *The Elements of Style*. New York: Macmillan, 1959.

SUNDQUIST, JAMES. *Making Federalism Work*. Washington, D.C.: Brookings Institution, 1969.

TURABIAN, KATE L. *A Manual for the Writers of Term Papers, Theses, and Dissertations*. 3d ed. Chicago: University of Chicago Press, 1969.

————. *Student's Guide for Writing College Papers*. 2d ed. Chicago: University of Chicago Press, 1969.

UNITED STATES NATIONAL ADVISORY COMMISSION ON CIVIL DISORDERS. *Report*. New York *Times* ed. New York: E. P. Dutton, 1968.

UNITED STATES NATIONAL ADVISORY COMMISSION ON CIVIL DISORDERS. *Supplemental Studies*. New York: Praeger, 1968.

UNITED STATES PRESIDENT'S COMMISSION ON LAW ENFORCEMENT AND THE ADMINISTRATION OF JUSTICE. *The Challenge of Crime in a Free Society*. Washington, D.C.: U.S. Government Printing Office, 1967.

UNIVERSITY OF CHICAGO PRESS. *A Manual of Style*. 12th ed. Chicago: University of Chicago Press, 1969.

VIDICH, ARTHUR, and JOSEPH BENSMAN. *Small Town in a Mass Society*. Garden City, N.Y.: Doubleday Anchor, 1960.

VIDICH, ARTHUR J., JOSEPH BENSMAN, and MAURICE R. STEIN. *Reflections on Community Studies*. New York: John Wiley and Sons, 1964.

WAHLKE, JOHN C., and others. *The Legislative System*. New York: John Wiley and Sons, 1962.

WALLACE, SAMUEL. *Skid Row as a Way of Life*. Totowa, N.J.: Bedminster Press, 1965.

WARNER, W. LLOYD, ed. *Yankee City*. New Haven, Conn.: Yale University Press, 1963.

WEINBERG, EVE. *Community Surveys with Local Talent: A Handbook*. Chicago: National Opinion Research Center, 1971.

WHITE, CARL M., and others. *Sources of Information in the Social Sciences: A Guide to the Literature.* Totowa, N.J.: Bedminster Press, 1964.

WHYTE, WILLIAM F. *Street Corner Society.* Chicago: University of Chicago Press, 1955.

WILDAVSKY, AARON. *The Politics of the Budgetary Process.* Boston: Little, Brown, 1964.

WILSON, JAMES. *Negro Politics.* New York: The Free Press, 1960.

WISEMAN, JACQUELINE, and MARCIA ARON. *Field Projects for Sociology Students.* San Francisco: Canfield Press, 1970.

INTRODUCTION TO ROLE PLAYING CASES (CHAPTERS 7–11)

ALTSHULER, ALAN. *The City Planning Process.* Ithaca, N.Y.: Cornell University Press, 1965.

————. *Community Control.* New York: Pegasus, 1970.

BANFIELD, EDWARD C. *Political Influence.* New York: The Free Press, 1961.

BERUBE, MAURICE, and MARILYN GITTELL. *Confrontation at Ocean Hill–Brownsville.* New York: Praeger, 1970.

BOLLENS, JOHN C., and HENRY J. SCHMANDT. *The Metropolis: Its People, Politics, and Economic Life.* 2d ed. New York: Harper and Row, 1970.

CLARK, KENNETH R. *A Relevant War on Poverty.* New York: Harper and Row, 1969.

DANIELSON, MICHAEL, ed. *Metropolitan Politics: A Reader.* 2d ed. Boston: Little, Brown, 1971.

DUHL, LEONARD, and NANCY JO STEELE. "Newark: Community or Chaos," *Journal of Applied Behavioral Science,* V (1969), 537–88.

DYE, THOMAS R., and BRETT W. HAWKINS, eds. *Politics in the Metropolis.* 2d ed. Columbus, Ohio: Charles E. Merrill, 1971.

EWALD, WILLIAM R., ed. *Environment for Man: The Next Fifty Years.* Bloomington: Indiana University Press, 1967.

GITTELL, MARILYN. *Participants and Participation.* New York: Praeger, 1967.

GOLDMAN, MARSHALL I., ed. *Controlling Pollution.* Englewood Cliffs, N.J.: Prentice-Hall, 1967.

GREER, SCOTT. *Urban Renewal and American Cities.* Indianapolis: Bobbs-Merrill, 1965.

KRAMER, RALPH. *Participation of the Poor: Comparative Case Studies in the War on Poverty.* Englewood Cliffs, N.J.: Prentice-Hall, 1969.

LEVITAN, SAR. *The Great Society's Poor Law.* Baltimore: Johns Hopkins Press, 1969.

MARRIS, PETER, and MARTIN REIN. *Dilemmas of Social Reform.* New York: Atherton Press, 1967.

MARSHALL, DALE ROGERS. *The Politics of Participation in Poverty.* Berkeley and Los Angeles: University of California Press, 1971.

MAYER, MARTIN. *The Teachers' Strike.* New York: Harper and Row, 1969.

MOYNIHAN, DANIEL PATRICK. *Maximum Feasible Misunderstanding.* New York: The Free Press, 1970.

OWEN, WILFRED. *The Metropolitan Transportation Problem,* rev. ed. Washington, D.C.: Brookings Institution, 1966.

RABINOVITZ, FRANCINE. *City Planning and Politics.* New York: Atherton Press, 1969.

ROGERS, DAVID. *110 Livingston Street.* New York: Vintage Books, 1969.

SCOTT, STANLEY, and JOHN C. BOLLENS. *Governing a Metropolitan Region: The San Francisco Bay Area.* Berkeley: University of California, Institute of Governmental Studies, 1968.

SUNDQUIST, JAMES. *Making Federalism Work.* Washington, D.C.: Brookings Institution, 1969.

SURKIN, MARVIN. "The Myth of Community Control." In Peter Orleans and William Russell Ellis, Jr., eds., *Race, Change, and Urban Society.* Beverly Hills: Sage Publications, 1971.

"Symposium on Collective Bargaining in the Public Service: A Reappraisal." *Public Administration Review,* XXXII (March/April 1972), 97–126.

"Symposium on Collective Negotiations in the Public Service." *Public Administration Review,* XXVIII (March/April 1968), 111–47.

UNITED STATES CONGRESS. SENATE COMMITTEE ON LABOR AND PUBLIC WELFARE. SUBCOMMITTEE ON EMPLOYMENT, MANPOWER, and POVERTY. *Examination of the War on Poverty: Staff and Consultant Reports.* 90th Congress, 1st Session, 1967.

UNITED STATES COUNCIL ON ENVIRONMENTAL QUALITY. *Environmental Quality.* Washington, D.C.: U.S. Government Printing Office, 1971.

WILSON, JAMES Q., ed. *The Metropolitan Enigma,* rev. ed. Cambridge, Mass.: Harvard University Press, 1968.

WINGO, LOWDON, ed. *The Governance of Metropolitan Regions.* Washington, D.C.: Resources for the Future, 1972.

ZAGORIA, SAM, ed. *Public Workers and Public Unions.* Englewood Cliffs, N.J.: Prentice-Hall, 1972.

ZIMMERMAN, JOSEPH F., ed. *Government of the Metropolis: Selected Readings.* New York: Holt, Rinehart and Winston, 1968.

index